LEADERSHIP IN BATTLE
1914-1918

Defence Is Our Business
Before the Dawn (Dunkirk and Burma)
The Only Enemy (autobiography)
Sandhurst
The Story of the Victoria Cross
The Story of the George Cross
In This Sign Conquer: The Story of the Army Chaplains
The Valiant
The Will to Live
Percival and the Tragedy of Singapore
Leadership in War 1939–1945

Leadership in Battle
1914–1918
COMMANDERS IN ACTION

Brigadier The Rt Hon
Sir John Smyth, Bt, VC, MC

D
521
S66
1976

DAVID & CHARLES · NEWTON ABBOT, LONDON, VANCOUVER

HIPPOCRENE BOOKS INC · NEW YORK

HIPPOCRENE
BOOKS, INC.

This edition first published in 1975 in Great Britain by
David & Charles (Holdings) Limited, Newton Abbot, Devon, and in
the United States of America in 1976 by Hippocrene Books Inc.,
New York
Published in Canada by Douglas, David & Charles Limited,
132 Philip Avenue, North Vancouver BC

ISBN 0 7153 7027 8 (Great Britain)

Library of Congress Cataloging in Publication Data
Smyth, John George, Sir, bart., 1893–
  Leadership in battle, 1914–1918
  Bibliography: p.
  1. European War, 1914–1918—Campaigns.
  2. Generals. I. Title.
/ D521.S66 1976   940.4'01   75–20132
  ISBN 0-88254-365-2

Set in Monotype Baskerville
and printed in Great Britain
by Latimer Trend & Company Ltd Plymouth

Contents

Illustrations

All photographs reproduced by courtesy of the Imperial War Museum, except the one marked with an asterisk, which is from a private collection

Introduction

I have often been asked to define leadership 'in a few words'. Difficult as that might appear to be, I think perhaps that is the only way in which one can define it. If one tries to list all the qualities a good leader must have one gets bogged down in an attempt to define a perfect person—who does not exist. A great leader must have courage, yet a very courageous person may not necessarily be a great leader. In a few words, a good leader is someone whom people will follow through thick and thin, in good times and in bad, because they have confidence in him as a persons in his ability and his knowledge of his job, perhaps because he looks the part, and also because his men know that they matter to him.

The confidence which men feel in their leader, in its turn, give, added confidence to the leader himself. It is an electric current working both ways. On the most momentous and frightening day of my life in the First World War, when I was asked to do something which we had all seen two other parties try to do, and fail—with no survivors—the most wonderful moment for me was when I asked for ten men to come with me—and the whole company volunteered. That gave me courage, and for me there was then no turning back. *Their* courage and confidence in me made me feel brave.

There are, of course, two kinds of leadership; there is leadership from the top at the general's level, and leadership in the lower ranks where example plays a big part. Both are indispensable for success in battle. The troops can't succeed if the plan is bad and the support is lacking—although there have been instances in our history where they have done so. But it is almost impossible for the most brilliant plan to succeed if the troops are deficient in courage, weapons and training.

In my book *Leadership in War 1939–1945* I wrote particularly of the generals of the Second World War, some of whom are still alive and most of whom I knew personally. It was a war of movement in which armoured fighting vehicles, lorried infantry and powerful air forces played a leading part. Even in the jungle it was the mobility and ubiquity of the Japanese which brought them their great initial victories on land in Malaya and Burma. And it was similar forces, better armed and used more intelligently, with much heavier air support, which enabled Slim's 14th Army to recapture Burma and destroy, first the mind, and then the body of the Japanese Army. The Second World War offered great scope for leadership on the part of the generals. The mobility conferred on them by car and aeroplane and much improved wireless communications enabled them to talk to the troops before, during and after battle, to show themselves to their men and to keep in much closer touch with the operations.

In the present book I have broadened my canvas by bringing in, at each period of the operations I am describing from the generals' aspect, some examples of leadership at the lower levels, and to this end I have quoted some of the Victoria Cross incidents of each period. In other words, how did the planning of the generals look and work out in the grim crucible of the battlefield and what did it entail for the troops?

Almost all the VCs I have known—and I have known a great many—have of course been proud of their highest decoration for gallantry, but humble in the knowledge that there were many others who deserved it as much as, or more than, they did. Nevertheless, every VC award demonstrated inspired leadership in some form, whether the man in question was only leading a platoon, or indeed operating by himself and in doing so setting an example which others might follow. From the point of view of the lower ranks the First World War, with its bitter close-quarter combat conditions of trench warfare in France and Gallipoli, brought more occasions when individual leadership and heroism were in evidence. No less than 633 VCs were awarded in the First World War as compared with 182 in the Second.

Leadership on the part of the generals was infinitely more difficult in the First World War than in the Second. In France, and to a lesser extent in Gallipoli, they were faced with a continuous line of trenches covered by vast acres of barbed wire. Surprise, the element which every commander strives to achieve in battle, was at a premium. Every offensive had to start with an attempt to break through this strong defensive system, which was flanked by well-concealed nests of Vickers machine-guns, the queens of the defensive battlefield. Such operations required a major build-up and the concentration of a great weight of artillery, infantry and air power—and even then in many cases the breakthrough was never attained. One reason was that the build-up required took weeks, if not months, to prepare, which made the all-powerful weapon of surprise difficult to acquire, if not impossible.

Even in the best-planned offensive it was impossible to guarantee that the enemy's wire and forward trench system would be completely put out of action by the preliminary bombardment; and in those sectors where this was not accomplished the attacking troops sustained fearful casualties. Why, then, the critics asked, was the attack not stopped in these sectors? It was this factor which was perhaps the chief cause of the bitterness and disillusionment which existed, and increased, as the war went on, on the part of the troops against the generals and the staff. The truth was that, with the crash of the artillery concentration throwing great mounds of earth into the air, the smoke and the cutting of all ground communications, the noise and the heavy casualties, a 'fog of war' descended on the battlefield which it often took some hours to penetrate.

Then, too, with the best will in the world a general's visit to the front-line trenches was apt to be unrewarding. Just before the battle of Neuve Chapelle in February 1915 I was acting as ADC to General Peter Strickland, who was then commanding the Jullundur Brigade in the Lahore Division. He was a tremendous tiger, who always liked to be as far forward in the battle as he could. He was anxious to pay a surprise visit to the front-line trenches to see what went on and to let the troops see him. I suggested that he should not wear his red-banded general's hat. This he at once turned down. 'How would they know who I was if they could not see who I was?'

We set off after breakfast in the brigade car. The approaches to our trench line were overlooked by the Germans, so we had to leave our car about two miles from the rear of the trench system— and even then we soon had to walk carefully as snipers were in action with both guns and rifles. Eventually we entered a long and narrow communication trench where every now and then there were warning notices of snipers. 'Keep your head down' they read; and we did. Soon we met traffic coming down the trench— some wounded and sick, fatigue parties, telephone linesmen, runners, etc. Passing was very difficult, and a general was clearly a perfect nuisance in a communication trench.

Our front-line trench was only 8oyd from the German front line. It was about a foot deep in mud and water. The men who had been on night duty were sleeping, some on the firestep, a few in dugouts. The others were going about the humdrum everyday tasks—cleaning rifles, getting the mud off their uniforms, foot inspections etc, delousing and writing letters back home. No opportunity at all for the general to say, à la Montgomery: 'Now gather round chaps and I'll tell you how the war is going.' There was nowhere to gather. They knew how their war was going and today was just another day, which might be acutely boring or much too exciting.

Passing along the trench was a difficult business. The general insisted on looking through one of the sentry's periscopes. The little flutter which this caused drew a sharp burst of fire from the German trench. We visited the CO of the battalion in his head-quarters dugout. He was rather offended that the general hadn't let him know he was coming. He told us that the Germans generally had a little hymn of hate about this time of day and suggested that the general should go before it started. The general, of course, insisted he would stay. The hymn of hate consisted of the firing of about half a dozen *minnenwerfer* mine-throwing mortars—'minnies' or 'portmanteaux' we used to call them. These missiles were each made of a steel drum packed with high explosive and scrap iron. You could see them turning over and over in the air in flight. The burning question was—where would they fall? They packed a terrific explosive charge but were not very accurate. In this case one of them landed close enough to blow in part of a trench and cause a number of casualties. We replied with a burst of mortar fire which was not so powerful but much more accurate. This elicited howls of rage from the German trench. We were told that, apart from the inevitable sniping which made leaving the trench for the purposes of nature—or any other purpose—precarious, this was probably the ration of hate for today.

And then of course at nightfall, with the trenches so close, and trench raids and patrolling on the tapis, everyone had to be on the qui vive. For the general it had been a long and exhausting day and he had a lot of work to do when he got back to his head-quarters. Was it worth it? Yes, I think for him it was but I don't think it made much impression on the troops. That was the sort of war it was.

General Strickland afterwards got command of a division and some six months later I had a most amusing letter from him from a London hospital. When the battle of Loos was planned he was determined to have his operational headquarters as near the front line as possible, instead of in some deep dugout at the back. So he had the inside of a large tree cut out to make himself a sort of 'machan', as for a tiger shoot in India. Before the battle started he and his GSO 1 climbed up the tree by a rope ladder, having had telephone lines laid on to Divisional HQ. But when the barrage started German guns and machine-guns opened up in reply and bullets started whizzing through the tree like a swarm of bees.

'I didn't admit I was wrong,' Strick said in his letter, 'until a bullet cut one rung of the rope ladder. Then I told the G 1 to get down. He was a very heavy man and the other rung of the ladder broke. I had to jump for it.' However, General Strickland was as hard as teak and it wasn't long before he was back with his division in France.

Despite all the difficulties the First World War did produce a number of fine battle leaders and the greatest of them was the Commander-in-Chief, Sir Douglas Haig, who was either in command of a corps or of the whole British Army from the first day of the war to the last—a fantastic achievement. He made mistakes, of course, and he had many critics as I shall show in this book. Prime Minister Lloyd George would have sacked him if he had had a bigger majority in the House of Commons and Haig had not had so much support from the army he commanded.

Douglas Haig was severely blamed for the Somme, that holocaust of British youth, in which the casualties were ghastly and by no means commensurate with the gains—which could only really be counted in the number of German casualties. But it must be remembered that Haig had never wanted to engage in the Somme battle. He was most averse to committing the new Kitchener Army divisions before they had been initiated properly into battle conditions. But, had he not done so, the French Army would have mutinied—as indeed it did at a later stage in the war. The French had bled themselves to death in their first offensives of the war when they thought that cold steel and courage could overcome the iron power of highly trained Germany infantry and artillery. But Haig continued his offensives too long and would have done better to adopt the 'bite and hold' policy of that very intelligent commander, Henry Rawlinson. Haig was also slow to discard his cavalry and concentrate on the new tanks—with which he finally won the war.

Where Haig did deserve most credit was in the fact that he was always at his best in a crisis. First Ypres in October 1914, the German breakthrough at Amiens in the Spring of 1918 (which so nearly won them the war), and our final offensive from August to November 1918, found him cool, confident and utterly in command of himself and his troops.

I came across him several times in the early part of the war.

He not only recommended me for the Victoria Cross but selected me, from a number of other VCs, to receive the first Russian Order of St George presented to his 1st Army by the Czar. I received this Order with a long letter from the Czar informing me that I was thereby entitled to free travel on all public transport in Russia and also to be an inspector of girls' schools. Alas, I never had the opportunity to take advantage of these facilities, and in the turmoil of battle I lost the Czar's valuable letter.

After the war I got to know two of the great army commanders of the First World War, who succeeded one another as commander-in-chief in India. They were Lord Rawlinson and Lord Birdwood. I became a personal friend of the latter and of his family. On his death I was invited by the BBC to broadcast an obituary to Australia.

There is no doubt that the First World War produced a glamour and a comradeship which exceeded anything in the Second. Most of the great war poetry and many of the great soldier songs came from the First World War. It is true that in the Second World War we had the wonderful comradeship of the 8th Army in the desert, and of the 14th Army in the jungle, from which stemmed the Burma Star Association, and the terrible ordeals of the Far Eastern prisoners of war, from which grew the Far Eastern Prisoner of War Association. It is noteworthy that it was from the sharing of hardships almost beyond human endurance that most of this comradeship sprang. In the First World War the most terrible hardships and slaughter were shared by so many and the comradeship which was forged then has endured to this day.

There was a school of thought, headed by Lloyd George, who thought we should reduce our troops in France and use them in other theatres. The result would have been fatal, because the Germans knew that the war would be won or lost on the Western Front; and Haig and Robertson, two confirmed 'Westerners', knew that the Germans knew this. Lloyd George's insistence that certain divisions should be diverted from France to Palestine early in 1918 nearly lost us the war as we were very short of troops when the big German *blitzkrieg* came in March 1918.

The First World War was essentially a war of people rather

than plans. 'The law was in the circumstances', and in the circumstances which existed the choice of plans was limited. What mattered was the way the plan was prepared and the guts, drive and sheer fortitude of the troops who had to carry it out. Leadership at all levels was worth much fine gold and Britain was fortunate in having the men for the job. But the generals have never had it so difficult and the PBI (Poor Bloody Infantry) have never had to show such grit—through the mud and the blood and the gas. They swore mightily and complained bitterly but their courage shone like a flame. I learnt more about leadership in 1914–15 in France than in the rest of my life put together.

I must admit, however, that the more I study the history and accounts of the First World War on the Western Front the more critical I become, not just of the generals but of the general plan on which some of the operations were based. My first criticism is with regard to the value put on the loss of ground, regardless of its tactical or strategical value. It was a sort of fetish that a trench or a trench system lost must be regained at all costs. Our counter-attacks at Ypres after the first use of gas by the Germans in April 1915 were a case in point. There was no great tactical value in the trenches we had lost, except that we had lost them. We could quite well have dug in where we were—and that is what we had to do in the end. But in the meantime we lost thousands of men—with a decline in our own morale and a boost to that of the Germans'—in trying to regain the captured trenches. My second criticism concerns major offensives like the Somme, which went on for weeks with quite terrible casualties and very few gains. Nearly all of these were due to failure on the opening day to cut the enemy wire and destroy his first-line defences. There were few instances of subsequent success when this had occurred, and the loss of morale and the bitterness on the part of the troops against the 'red tabs' of the generals and the staff were definite drawbacks and obstacles to our final victory.

I have explained the difficulties facing the generals earlier in this introduction and I shall refer to them again later. But, even allowing for them, I think there was much too much rigidity of planning and too little brain. Instead of the artillery concentrations and barrages, on which the whole operation depended, working up to a crescendo, after which the infantry at once assaulted —only to find in some cases, and in some sectors of the attack, that the wire was uncut and the front-line trenches heavily manned—it might have been better for the artillery preparation to have had stops in it to allow for some inspection of the damage done, and also to get the defending infantry to leave their dugouts and man the trenches where they could then have been deluged with shrapnel. I know all the difficulties and was on the receiving end of some of them. In the pauses, of course, the enemy might have been able to repair damage to the wire—but not if the pauses were made only in daylight. I have no doubt at all that in a big planned attack it would have been better for the attack in some sectors not to have gone in at all, or to have been postponed until the next day rather than risk the awful shambles of the Somme and Passchendaele.

My third criticism of the generals' strategy is that the 'bite and hold' plan advocated by General Rawlinson might well have been adopted more often rather than the so-called 'au fond' operation favoured by General Joffre for the Somme.

In the end, of course, final victory was gained by the British in France by a combination of a short, pulverising bombardment, followed immediately by the tanks. The Allied programme for 1919, had it become necessary, was based on the same policy but with hundreds more tanks of the latest pattern. The Second World War began where the first left off; but this time with the Germans bursting through and nullifying the greatest defence system the world had ever seen, the Maginot Line, and driving deep with their panzers into the heart of France. In both cases the first military principle of surprise came into its own again.

CHAPTER ONE

The Start of the War in France

The mobilisation of the British Expeditionary Force, under the command of Field-Marshal Sir John French, began on the day war was declared, 4 August 1914. By 20 August four divisions, the cavalry division and two additional brigades, one cavalry and one infantry, were concentrated on the left of the French Army between Mauberge and Le Cateau. However, the 4th Infantry Division arrived to join them on 22 August and the 6th Division on 9 September.

As soon as war had been declared the Government decided that Lord Kitchener should become Secretary of State for War and he took up his duties immediately. Whilst nearly all the political and military pundits were forecasting that the war would be a short one, Kitchener was quite convinced that it would be a long, all-out struggle, and he made plans accordingly for a vast recruiting and training programme. He was not convinced that the arrangement made by General Wilson with General Foch for the employment of the BEF in the opening stages of the war was the best one. He would have kept the BEF farther back, and he may well have been right. But he realised that the plan which had been made could not be altered at the last minute. He did, however, insist that the 4th and 6th Divisions should be retained for home defence until all danger of invasion had passed.

The two BEF corps commanders were Sir Douglas Haig (1

Corps) and Sir Horace Smith-Dorrien (2 Corps). The latter had
replaced Sir James Grierson who had died from a heart attack on
his way up to Mons. Grierson, aged fifty-five, had been considered
one of the two most experienced and capable generals in the Army.
Moreover he was a personal friend of French and Haig. French
had at once asked Kitchener to send out Sir Herbert Plumer in
his place, but Kitchener had sent Smith-Dorrien. French, not
unnaturally, took this as a slight as he knew the senior officers in
the Army a great deal better than Kitchener. So from the start
an unfortunate rift made itself felt in the relations between the
C-in-C and the Secretary of State.

Sir John French was a cavalry soldier who had added to his
already high reputation by his leadership of the cavalry in the
South African War and was marked out for high advancement.
He had graduated to the highest peacetime appointment in the
Army, Chief of the Imperial General Staff, via the most important
peacetime command of troops, the Aldershot Command. Short
and square in build, but carrying a bit too much weight, he was
now in his sixty-second year and appeared to be well past his
best, both physically and mentally. There were doubts in some
quarters as to whether he had the qualifications for high command
in a continental war.

Douglas Haig, on his way out to France, had expressed severe
criticism of French to Charteris, his Military Secretary and future
Chief of Intelligence Staff. Haig considered French to be unversed
in the strategy of modern warfare and too obstinate to accept the
views of others. And he had written in his diary on 11 August:
'I know that French is quite unfit for this great command at a
time of crisis in our country's history.' He did, however, give
French credit for his good tactical powers, his great courage and
his determination. Haig wrote equally disparagingly of French's
staff at GHQ.

So what with the slight difference of opinion between Kitchener
and French over a successor to General Grierson, French's
lukewarm acceptance of Smith-Dorrien, and Haig's rather low
opinion of his commander-in-chief, there were already rifts in the
lute which widened as the operations progressed.

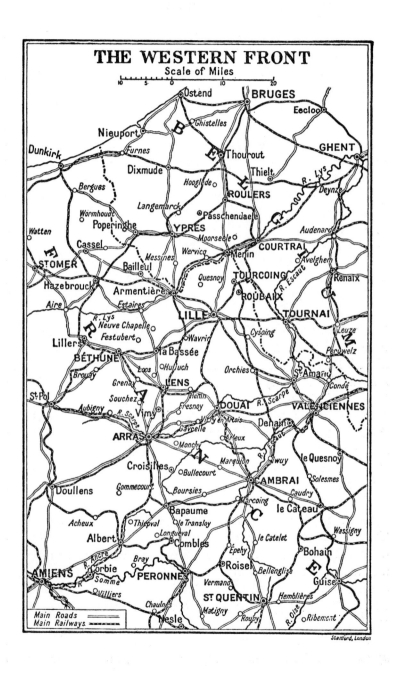

THE WESTERN FRONT

Scale of Miles

Ostend · BRUGES · Eecloo
Nieuport · Ghistelles · GHENT
Dunkirk · Furnes · Thourout · Thielt
Dixmude · Hooglede · R. Lys · Deynze
Bergues · Langemarck · ROULERS
Wormhoudt · Poperinghe · Passchendaele · Audenarde
Watten · Cassel · YPRES · Moorseele · COURTRAL
STOMER · Bailleul · Wervicq · Menin · Avelghem · Renaix
Hazebrouck · Messines · Quesnoy · TOURCOING
Armentières · ROUBAIX · TOURNAI
Aire · Estaires · LILLE · Leuze
Neuve Chapelle · Wavrin · Cysoing · Peruwelz
Lillers · Festubert · la Bassée · Orchies · St Amand · Condé
BÉTHUNE · Loos · Hulluch · VALENCIENNES
Brouay · Grenay · LENS · DOUAI · Denain
St Pol · Souchez · Henin · R. Scarpe
Aubigny · Vimy · Fresnoy · Vitry en Artois · le Quesnoy
ARRAS · Gavrelle · Arleux · Iwuy · Solesmes
Monchy · Marquion · CAMBRAI · Caudry
Croisilles · Bullecourt · le Cateau
Doullens · Gommecourt · Boursies · Marcoing · le Cateau
Bapaume · Wassigny
Acheux · Thiepval · le Transloy · le Catelet · Bohain
Albert · Longueval · Épehy
Combles · Roisel · Bellenglise · Guise
AMIENS · Orbie · Bray · PERONNE · Vermand · Hemblières
Somme · Villiers · St QUENTIN
Chaulnes · Matigny · Rouoy · R. Oise · Ribemont
Nesle

Main Roads
Main Railways

Stanford, London

Douglas Haig had certainly had a most distinguished career and one eminently fitted for his high appointment as corps commander. Aged fifty-three, eight years younger than French, he was a handsome, strongly built man who had always kept himself in prime condition, both physically and mentally. He was born at Edinburgh in 1861 and was educated at Clifton and became an undergraduate of Brasenose College, Oxford in 1880. It was there that he became a good horseman and learned to play polo, which was the only game at which he excelled—and excelled is the word. In August 1886 he was selected to play polo for England against America when the Americans were defeated by ten goals to four and then by fourteen goals to two. These were indeed great days for English polo.

Haig was a popular young man and was quite well off. He was also a man of strong character and determined to succeed in anything he undertook. As it appeared that he had already made up his mind to go into the Army, it is curious that he did not go to Sandhurst instead of Oxford. However, when he came down from Oxford in 1883 he went to an Army crammer to prepare himself for the Sandhurst examination, which he was allowed to take at a later age by reason of his graduation at Oxford. Though he lost seniority by this procedure he had the advantage of starting his Army career with a wider education and general knowledge than most of the young military officers of his generation. At Sandhurst he threw himself wholeheartedly into his military studies and, in December 1884, he passed out first and was awarded the Anson Memorial Sword as Senior Under-Officer. In February 1885 he was commissioned in the 7th Hussars.

In 1893, after many months of study, Haig sat for the Staff College examination—and failed. This was really the only set-back in his military career. He returned to his regiment in India and took the examination again three years later. This time he passed, and he entered Camberley in 1896. He then applied to serve with the Egyptian Army and saw service with Kitchener in the Sudan, including the battle of Omdurman.

In the South African War (October 1899–1902) Haig was appointed Chief of Staff to Sir John French, who was selected to command the cavalry in Natal. In that position Haig earned high praise from Sir John and after the relief of Kimberley he was appointed Chief Staff Officer (AAG) to the Cavalry Division of four brigades—an important appointment indeed.

Haig left South Africa with a very high reputation. French, who had become Commander-in-Chief at Aldershot, was anxious that he should command his cavalry brigade; but Kitchener, who had become Commander-in-Chief in India, was equally determined to secure his services as Inspector General of Cavalry; and it was to the latter appointment that Haig went. Never before had a British officer of such junior rank been given such an important position in the British Army in India.

Before sailing Haig was invited to Balmoral, where King Edward VII presented him with the CVO as a 'mark of personal esteem'. This somewhat unusual award for a comparatively junior cavalry officer who had no particular connection with the Palace was significant in view of the fact that, in later years when he met with criticism as commander-in-chief in France, he was always credited with having the ear and support of the king. It was whilst he was staying at Windsor Castle in 1905 that Haig met his future wife, Miss Dorothy Vivian.

Haig's next appointment was as Director of Military Training at the War Office, in which post he was to play a leading part in the reforms which the new Secretary of State, Lord Haldane, was planning. And in the three years which followed, Haig did much to assist in preparing the British Army for war.

In 1909 O'Moore Creagh, the newly appointed commander-in-chief in India, invited Haig to go to India as his chief of staff. Haig felt that this would give him a break and also new experience and he decided to accept. Whilst he was in Delhi he took a particular interest in the new Staff College at Quetta and also gave his attention to a plan for the possible movement of troops from India to Europe in the event of war. And how important that turned out to be!

In May 1911 Haig was offered the Aldershot Command which was shortly to be vacated by Sir Horace Smith-Dorrien. This was the most important command in Britain, and Haig was very glad to accept—particularly as it gave him promotion over a number of other general officers.

Smith-Dorrien was born in 1858 and was thus fifty-six when the war started, three years older than Haig. He was educated at Harrow and then, after a period at a crammer's, he passed into Sandhurst in 1878. In those days he got a year's ante-date of seniority by getting a special mention for particularly meritorious work. Thus he passed out of the college seven years earlier than Haig and had gained considerably in seniority from not going to Oxford.

Smith-Dorrien first saw service in the Zulu War in 1879 and was actually in Isandhlwana camp when, in broad daylight, it was overrun by a large force of Zulus on 22 January. Smith-Dorrien made a miraculous escape and eventually arrived at Rorke's Drift just after the heroic defence of the post by the 1st Bn 24th (South Wales Borderers) in which that battalion gained the record number of seven VCs in one day.

Having seen more active service with the Egyptian Army, Smith-Dorrien passed into the Staff College in 1887. He much enjoyed his two years there, was Master of the Drag and revelled in the hunting and steeple-chasing. He was a splendid horseman. Later he did a lot of race-riding in India and was the winner of many races. He took part in the Tirah Campaign of 1897–8 and then the Egyptian Campaign which followed. Then came the South African War in which Smith-Dorrien much distinguished himself; and he was promoted major-general on 11 February 1900 and posted to India as Adjutant-General at Army Head-quarters. Later he was given command of the 4th Division in Quetta (Baluchistan). Then, in 1907, he was given the Aldershot Command. Except for his two years at the Staff College he had not done a day's duty in the UK for twenty-seven years.

To have been given the Aldershot Command is in itself sufficient recommendation of Smith-Dorrien as one of the most highly regarded leaders in the British Army. He had followed Sir John French in this appointment and preceded Douglas Haig. Smith-Dorrien's chief of staff at Aldershot was 'Wully' Robertson, whose biographer, Victor Bonham-Carter, says in his book, *Soldier True*:

At that time Aldershot was still the principal training ground of the Army with two infantry divisions (Grierson had one), one cavalry brigade and a number of ancillary units. Facilities were only fair, but much hard and imaginative training was done, thanks to Wully's efficiency and to the drive and foresight of the GOC, Smith-Dorrien. The latter was not easy to get on with. He suffered from attacks of gout in the head, when he was liable to give vent to fearful explosions of temper. But these were minor afflictions, for in truth Smith-Dorrien was an excellent commander. He cared deeply for the well-being of the private soldier. He treated everyone, whatever his rank, as an individual capable of thinking for himself. In training he insisted on self-reliance and intelligent discipline, no less than on proficiency in fieldcraft and the ability to handle a rifle.

In fact Wully thought very highly of him—and Wully was a very stern critic.

In 1912 Smith-Dorrien became a full general. Then, following the sudden death of Grierson, he was ordered out to France as General Officer Commanding 2 Corps.

The short orders which Kitchener had given to Sir John French were to the effect that he should make every effort to co-operate with the French in accordance with the plans already made but that his command was entirely independent and he would not come under the orders of any Allied general. Whether or not Sir John French was the general best qualified to command the BEF in this desperate venture, he was certainly involved at once in operations of enormous anxiety and complexity, which would have tested any British commander who had ever lived and from which he was lucky to have extricated his troops with such credit that they could turn and fight back when the opportunity offered.

Winston Churchill once wrote about the start of the First World War: 'No part of the Great War compares in interest with its opening, the first collision was a drama never surpassed and all that happened afterwards consisted of battles which, however formidable, were but desperate and vain appeals against the decision of fate.' It was quite different and much more dramatic than the Second World War in that, by some ten years before 1914, the general staffs of the main combatants—the Germans, the French, the Russians and the British—had more or less completed their plans of battle. Germany always intended to invade France by a giant right-wing sweep through Belgium. France, intent above all else on regaining Alsace and Lorraine, planned an all-out direct offensive to that end. Russia planned a pincer invasion of East Prussia, while the German armies were involved in the West. And Britain, through military conversations originated by Foch and Henry Wilson, committed her small army to co-operation with France.

For at least five years before the war started each of these continental general staffs knew what the others planned to do, down to the last detail. And yet none of them changed their own plan in any way to counter the offensive of the other. This applied particularly to Germany and France. It was the most extraordinary military set-up on a vast scale that the world has ever seen, or is ever likely to see.

Clausewitz, who had the same influence on German military thinking at that time as Liddell Hart had later on the British, was an almost fanatical advocate of the *blitzkrieg*. He decreed that to gain victory by an early decisive battle was the outstanding object in any war. Curiously enough, the French had just the same conviction before the First World War but they didn't write so much about it. They did, however, teach it most emphatically at their Staff College and in all their military exercises.

The French and Germans differed in their implementation of this theory in that the French adopted the 'attaque brusque'—the head-on confrontation—whereas the Germans aimed at getting an equally decisive result by crushing the flanks of their enemy. The German was the more effective plan in modern war, as indeed it had been in other wars. It was, in fact, Liddell Hart's theory of 'the indirect approach'.

CHAPTER TWO

The Retreat from Mons
and the Battle of Le Cateau

The first skirmishes of the war brought the award of the first
Victoria Crosses. Everyone's hopes were high and no one yet
imagined the form that the war was about to take. Young men were
filled with dreams of gallantry, of dash and the opportunity to
do great deeds. They still thought in terms of a war of movement.

The first Victoria Cross of the war was won at Mons by Lieutenant M. J. Dease of the 4th Battalion Royal Fusiliers on Sunday,
23 August. On the next day, at Audregnies, Belgium, the sixth
VC of the war was won by Captain Francis Grenfell of the 9th
Lancers. The 9th Lancers, with the 4th Dragoon Guards and the
18th Hussars, made up the 2nd Cavalry Brigade. On 21 August
the 9th had moved to Hermignies, four miles south-east of Mons,
and had their first sight of the war. A patrol sent out to the canal
bridges north of Mons caught a glimpse of Uhlans in the distance.
What a thrill for the patrol—and probably a great surprise for the
Uhlans.

Late on the night of the 22nd the regiment received orders to
move across the rear of the British Army, from the right flank to
the left, and take post at Thulin, nine miles south-west of the
Mons–Valenciennes road, in support of the left of 2 Corps, which
was holding the line of the Mons–Condé canal. The horses slid
and stumbled along the *pavé* roads in the pitch darkness, but

although there were several falls no man or horse was seriously hurt.

At last, just before dawn on the 23rd, the regiment halted in a wet field south of Thulin. Soon after midday the sound of gun and rifle fire from the north announced that British infantry were engaged with the Germans along the line of the Mons Canal. It was the first battle of the war and the regiment found itself in anything but ideal cavalry country—densely populated, with coalmines, smoky villages, towering slag heaps, railway embankments and endless wire fences.

After various rumours that Uhlans had been reported in the vicinity, the whole of 2 Cavalry Brigade mounted and rode off in search of them. But no Uhlans were discovered. Captain Francis Grenfell, B Squadron, with a troop of A Squadron in support, remained on outpost duty. Next morning, the 24th, the 9th Lancers ran into advancing German infantry and withdrew on to the main body of the 2nd Cavalry Brigade. The brigade was then ordered to return and take action against the German 4 Corps, which was threatening to envelop the 5th Division, the left division of 2 Corps. The situation became critical for 5 Div, and the 9th Lancers and 4th Dragoon Guards were ordered to charge across country cut up by sunken lanes, railway cuttings and quickset hedges and covered with corn stooks, behind which German infantry were in position. The cavalry swept over a sunken road, spearing one or two Germans before being struck by shell fire and a hail of bullets. Losing men at every stride, they suddenly came up against a long wire fence. Men and horses fell in all directions.

This charge was as futile and gallant as other attempts in history when cavalry have charged unbroken infantry—and in country which could hardly have been more unfavourable for mounted action.

Francis Grenfell, left as senior officer, rallied part of the 9th Lancers behind a railway embankment but he was hit twice and severely wounded. The commander of the 119th Field Battery, Lieut-Colonel E. W. Alexander, appealled to Francis Grenfell to help him to save his guns. Grenfell at once responded and, with a party of eleven volunteers from the 9th, together with Alexander and some dozen gunners, they ran across two fields and man-handled the guns back under cover. The guns had to be turned and lifted over the dead bodies of the gun teams under heavy fire. The horses and drivers were then able to gallop the guns away to safety. Despite his wounds, Captain Grenfell rode nearly ten miles back with the remains of his squadron before collapsing from exhaustion. Both he and Colonel Alexander were awarded the Victoria Cross.

Two months later Francis Grenfell was wounded again in a desperate encounter in which the 9th suffered heavy casualties, particularly in officers. He was invalided home and had his Cross presented to him by the king on 21 February 1915. But he was eager to get back to his regiment and left again for the front as soon as he was allowed to do so, on 17 April.

This desire amongst so many of Britain's finest young men to return to the fighting was a very marked characteristic of the early years of the war. Men said despairingly: 'The war will be over before I get there.' The war came to many as a great crusade in which they would find the verities. This great upsurge of feeling was well expressed by Rupert Brooke in his poem 'Peace':

Now God be thanked who has matched us with His hour,
And caught our youth, and wakened us from sleeping.
With hands made sure, clear eye, and sharpened power,
To turn, as swimmers into cleanness leaping,
Glad from a world grown old and cold and weary,
Leave the sick hearts that honour could not move,
And half-men, and their dirty songs and dreary,
And all the little emptiness of love!

Francis Grenfell returned to France and went through all the grim fighting at and near Ypres in April and May and on 24 May was mortally wounded and died a few minutes later. His twin brother Riversdale—'Rivy'—had already been killed with the 9th a few months earlier. They were splendid young officers, born leaders of men, whom Britain could ill spare at this critical time—and they were typical of so many.

On Sunday, 23 August, the Germans had advanced with dramatic suddenness against the British Expeditionary Force which, only two days earlier, had arrived to hold the line of the Mons Canal with 2 Corps on the left and 1 Corps on the right. Fighting was severe from Obourg westwards almost to Condé, the German attacks in massed formations being heavily punished by the accurate and rapid musketry fire of the British infantry. In these early engagements 2 Corps bore the brunt of the fighting. However, owing to the alarming news received that evening concerning the French armies on his right, Field-Marshal Sir John French ordered a general retirement of the BEF, which was already somewhat in advance of its allies and would otherwise have been in danger of being cut off.

On Monday, 24 August, therefore, the historic 'Retreat from Mons' began. 1 Corps (1st and 2nd Divisions under Haig) fell back westwards of Mauberge, covered by 2 Corps (3rd and 4th Divisions under Smith-Dorrien). After heavy fighting the latter withdrew by nightfall and bivouacked in the neighbourhood of Bavai, with 1 Corps on his right. An awkward problem then arose when the two corps approached the Forest of Mormal, thickly wooded, nine miles long and four miles wide. There were a number of roads which crossed the forest from east to west but none that ran down it from north to south. To have attempted to pass both corps down one side of the forest would have entailed considerable crowding and confusion and would also have placed additional strain on the rearguards and on the cavalry, who were hard put to it to hold off the rapidly advancing Germans. Sir John French therefore decided, quite rightly, but with considerable trepidation, to divide his army and send 1 Corps to the east of the forest and 2 Corps to the west. As it turned out, their separation was to be a long one and packed with great events.

On the 25th the retirement continued. It must be remembered that, before the retreat started, the British troops had been compelled to carry out long forced marches from their derailment stations to the forward concentration areas; they then had to move forward to the Mons Canal and dig themselves in. Almost immediately they were called upon to leave their entrenchments and undertake long and disheartening retreats, for which they could see no reason—nor could their commanders very well give them any reason except that the French had been forced back on their right and the British had to conform. All these things had put a great strain on the supply services and entailed nightmare changes of plan for the already overworked staff at GHQ.

The extremely hot weather and the hard cobbled roads were very trying for men and horses alike. It must be remembered also that half the men were reservists just called up and not in hard condition. Many of the horses also, particularly in the artillery batteries, were remounts and already very much the worse for wear with continuous work on the hard *pavé* roads, with little rest and scanty food.

Meanwhile a welcome reinforcement reached the BEF in the shape of the 4th Division, which had arrived west of Le Cateau and, on 25 August, moved towards Solesnes to join 2 Corps.

The day of 25 August proved an exhausting one for 2 Corps. There was great congestion on the roads from refugees and French cavalry passing across their front. The 5th Division on the right had withdrawn along the Roman road on the western side of the Forest of Mormal. During this seven-mile stretch the heat had been scorching, particularly as the great trees prevented any breeze from reaching the tired troops. The constant checks, frequent deployments and then reforming, and continuous marching, all on very short rations for men and horses, were most trying for the rearguard battalions and their supporting artillery batteries—most of all for the latter as they had continually to be taking up covering positions and then limbering up again. In the 3rd Division, 7 Infantry Brigade, on rearguard, reached their bivouacs at a very late hour. Even then some of the units had not arrived and the divisional commander did not think the men would be fit to go on again until 9 am at the earliest. The 4th Division were in much the same plight; 5 Div, though less exhausted, were more scattered.

It was quite late in the evening before Smith-Dorrien received complete situation reports from his subordinate commanders and it then became clear to him that, unless his troops could continue their withdrawal during the night of 25/26 August they would become sorely pressed by the Germans when they continued their retreat on the 26th and a very serious situation might result. As all the divisional commanders were emphatic that neither men nor horses could continue until 9 am next day at the earliest, there appeared to be no other alternative but to stand and fight, give the Germans a knock and then continue the withdrawal. General Allenby (commanding the Cavalry Division) arrived at Smith-Dorrien's headquarters at 2 am on the 26th and agreed with the divisional commanders' conclusions. He said that unless he moved by night he might find difficulty in getting away at all and his men and his horses were very tired.

Smith-Dorrien then asked Allenby if he would co-operate with him and take his orders if he stood at Le Cateau and attempted to 'give the Germans a bloody nose' before continuing the withdrawal. When Allenby agreed, Smith-Dorrien at once issued his orders accordingly. Even so there was little enough time to get the orders out and in many cases the infantry and the artillery had to take up positions from the map, without any time for reconnaissance on the ground, some of which turned out to be unsuitable. However, once more the 'law was in the circumstances' and they could only do their best. Although GHQ were not happy about his decision Smith-Dorrien realised that, if he didn't stand, the German advanced guards would be right on top of his weary retreating troops early next day and a major disaster might result which would affect 1 Corps as much as his own. It must be emphasised that at this time Smith-Dorrien imagined that 1 Corps would be on his right and would be holding the high ground east of Le Cateau, whence an enemy could enfilade a considerable portion of his line. This belief was, of course, shared by 5 Div, on the right of the defence line of 2 Corps, the formation most affected.

Having issued his orders Smith-Dorrien reported his action to GHQ at St-Quentin by sending an officer in a car. Sir John French wisely concurred—he could hardly do anything else—but asked Smith-Dorrien to continue his retreat as soon as possible. Where Sir John's staff fell down very badly was that they didn't

Page 33 (*above left*) Field-Marshal Sir John French, Commander-in-Chief BEF; (*above right*) General Sir Horace Smith-Dorrien, the hero of Le Cateau; (*below*) General Joffre, President Poincaré, HM the King, General Foch, Sir Douglas Haig, at GHQ France, 12 August 1916

Page 34 (*above left*) Marshal Foch with General Sir William Robertson; (*above right*) Captain Carton de Wiart, VC, 4th Dragoon Guards, France 1916; (*below*) HM the King with British Army Commanders at Buckingham Palace, 19 December 1918. Left to right: Birdwood, Rawlinson, Plumer, HM the King, Haig, Horne, Byng

inform Douglas Haig! Smith-Dorrien believed that 1 Corps was prolonging his right flank at Le Cateau whereas Haig continued his withdrawal in the very early hours of the 26th, thinking that 2 Corps was doing the same. And at 8 pm that evening he telegraphed to GHQ: 'No news of 2 Corps except sound of guns from direction of Le Cateau and Beaumont. Can 1 Corps be of any assistance?'

To this message GHQ made no reply and even on the morning of the 27th 1 Corps knew nothing of the heroic battle fought by 2 Corps at Le Cateau the previous day. How extraordinary it seems to us in these days of aeroplanes, helicopters and R/T that these two corps, only seven miles apart, should have been so completely out of touch with one another and that GHQ, which had only just left Le Cateau, was so completely unaware of the situation. It seems incredible that GHQ never told 2 Corps that 1 Corps intended to move early on the 26th or told 1 Corps that 2 Corps intended to stand and fight at Le Cateau.

The position on which Smith-Dorrien decided to fight was from Le Cateau to Esnes, a front about thirteen miles in extent. This was to be held by the 5th, 3rd and 4th Divisions, 5 Div on the right. The total number of troops at Smith-Dorrien's disposal was 12 cavalry regiments, 2 squadrons of divisional cavalry, and 40 infantry battalions, and he had 246 guns. 4 Div, however, was without its divisional cavalry on 26 August. Each cavalry regiment and infantry battalion had two machine-guns, but several of these had been destroyed at Mons on 23 and 24 August.

The Germans employed part of four corps at Le Cateau and two cavalry divisions. They had, therefore, an enormous superiority in numbers and had about three times as many guns and machine-guns—and they used these very boldly.

Drenching rain had started at 5.00 pm on the 25th and continued until midnight. The bivouacs occupied that evening were sodden and cheerless and the day of 26 August, the anniversary of the battle of Crécy, dawned hot and misty. The change of plan made by the corps commander took some time to filter down to the troops. The result was that some of the gun positions, selected to support a further withdrawal, were too close to the infantry

c

positions for a defensive battle. However, as it turned out, the proximity of their supporting artillery gave the British infantry great confidence although it made things dangerous for the gunners serving the guns—a situation they readily accepted. The 5th Division suffered a set-back on their right flank almost before the battle started as the battalions of 14 Infantry Brigade, which lay west of Le Cateau, did not receive their counter-orders to stand fast until about 6.00 am. They were therefore caught on the move by the German advanced guards pressing forward under cover of the early morning mist. Thus a dangerous situation developed which became more and more critical as the day wore on and exposed 15 Brigade Royal Field Artillery and the infantry they were supporting to damaging enfilade fire. This situation, of course, could not have occurred if, as the corps commander and 5 Div commander believed, 1 Corps had been holding the high ground on their right.

Everywhere the British infantry and their supporting gunners were putting up a terrific fight, the latter getting in some splendid targets against the massed German infantry. But it was on the exposed right flank that the chief danger developed. And here 15 Brigade Group RFA acquitted itself with great heroism, continuing to keep its guns in action whilst there was a man left to man them.

The action of 15 Brigade RFA in this historic engagement is worth recording in further detail. The brigade consisted of three 18pdr batteries, each of three sections, each section having two guns. Each gun had a firing battery wagon, which stayed in the wagon lines with the gun limbers until required. The battery officers were a major, a captain and three section commanders (subalterns). The 18pdrs had an extreme range of 6,500yd.

For the battle of Le Cateau the Commander Royal Artillery had put 37 (Howitzer) Battery from 8 Medium Brigade under command of 15 Brigade. The howitzers had an extreme range of 6,000yd. The 15 Brigade commander was Lieut-Colonel C. F. Stevens. The three battery commanders were Major Henning (11 Bty), Major Nutt (52 Bty), and Major Birley (80 Bty). 37 Bty was commanded by Major Jones.

The four batteries of 15 Brigade (from right to left, 11, 80, 37, 52) came into action immediately behind the infantry front line and actually in front of the infantry who were in support of this section of the front. Only 37 Battery had time to dig in before the enemy shell and rifle fire opened. Practically all the other three batteries could do was to camouflage the guns by fastening cornstooks on the gun shields.

The 2nd Suffolks had taken up their position in front of 15 Brigade, with the 2nd Manchesters behind them in brigade reserve, and there were two companies of the East Surreys on the right of the Suffolks. Soon after 5 am the German artillery opened fire. 15 Brigade and 37 Battery replied at once, engaging the gun flashes at a range of about 5,000yd and silencing two of the enemy batteries. But the Germans, bringing more guns into action, subjected 15 Brigade to a very heavy and accurate fire, mostly high explosive but partly shrapnel. This caused a number of casualties in the gun detachments, and also among the Suffolks, who took several shells intended for the batteries. The enemy had the sun behind them, which was a considerable advantage.

At 6.50 am a salvo of high explosive burst on 15 Brigade's observation post. The Brigade Commander, Lieut-Colonel Stevens, sustained a painful wound in the spine but remained at duty. Major Jones, commanding 37 Battery, Captain Leach, the adjutant, and the battery sergeant-major of 37 Battery were all struck by shell fragments but remained at duty. All battery wagon lines had to move more than once and their losses were heavy, particularly in horses. 11 Battery lost 58, 52 Battery lost 102, 80 Battery lost 70 and 37 Battery lost 50.

At about 9.45 am our airmen reported a column of enemy infantry, six miles long, entering Englefontaine. 15 Brigade and 37 Battery took them on at ranges which were as low as 900yd. Meanwhile, at 52 Battery observation post, Sergeant Woolger was killed and the battery sergeant-major wounded. 11 Battery was engaged by German artillery from the front and from the right flank and two of their officers became casualties. The enemy artillery fire was increasing all the time. But the battery commander, Major Henning, continued observing coolly from the centre of his battery as he could not maintain telephone communication from his original OP. The left section was then manhandled back with the help of some men of the Manchester Regiment to take on the guns enfilading them from the right flank. Lieutenant Stamford, the Left Section commander, was soon hit and Captain Buckle then directed the fire of these three guns until he was mortally wounded. The fire of these three guns, at point-blank range, together with the devastating effect produced by the rifles and machine-guns of the Manchesters, relieved the pressure from this most dangerous quarter. But 11 Battery's casualties had been heavy. Eventually the battery commander, Major Henning, was the only officer surviving and he was wounded in the knee by a piece of shrapnel. However, he kept one gun in action until about noon, engaging any target that appeared.

Immediately to the left of 11 Battery, 80 Battery (Major Birley), although enfiladed from both flanks, remained in action and maintained a heavy and accurate fire on any German infantry that appeared. But ammunition began to run low, so Captain Higgon brought up three wagons, two of which got through. Captain Higgon remained up with the guns, as did Lieutenant Hewson, despite the fact that he was wounded. Major Birley had set a splendid example to his gunners and gained the admiration of the Suffolks. He walked about the battery all day, observing fire, entirely regardless of his own safety. He had lost one subaltern, Lieutenant McLeod, early on, but Lieutenant Mirrless remained unscathed.

On his right flank the guns were less than 100yd behind the Suffolks' trenches, whilst on the left, 200yd separated them. There was now a deafening noise of artillery fire from the guns of both the Germans and the British. 37 Battery, which had been engaged in shelling distant columns of German infantry, now turned on their advancing waves at closer ranges, until gradually it expended nearly all the ammunition in both its wagon lines. 52 Battery, the left battery of 15 Brigade, fought in the open under extremely heavy fire. Before it had been definitely located it had punished two German batteries very severely. But gradually casualties mounted. Major Nutt, the battery commander, was shot clean through the throat and fainted. When he came round he continued to control his battery, although he could only speak in a whisper.

Now the enemy artillery fire increased and ever greater numbers of German infantry were joining in the attack. As 3 Cavalry Brigade and 14 Infantry Brigade were forced off the Le Cateau spur the British right flank was entirely in the air. German action on this exposed flank was, for a time, confined to artillery fire in preparation for a fresh infantry attack. It was estimated that over 100 German guns, besides the many machine-guns, were massed against the Suffolks and 15 Brigade RFA. This concentrated fire gradually wore down 15 Brigade. In No 11 Battery only the Number 2 gun was firing. 80 Battery's detachment was reduced to two or three men and both batteries suffered severely from the German 4·2in howitzers on the exposed right flank. 37 Battery still had all its guns in action, chiefly owing to the fact that they had greater cover in front and to their right and had been able to dig in, whilst the other three batteries were changing their original positions. In 52 Battery only the flank guns were firing. During the day this battery alone had fired over 1,000 rounds.

By 1.45 pm the Germans had brought many machine-guns into action along the Cambrai road and the right flank of 5 Div was under severe pressure. They informed 2 Corps that unless this was soon diminished there was a grave risk that the right flanks might give way. But when the German infantry attempted to force their way through they met with such a warm reception that they reverted to massive artillery action. However, although they were hesitant in making a direct assault upon the British infantry—for whom they now had considerable respect—they were steadily pouring round the open right flank of the Suffolks and 15 Brigade RFA. 2 Corps ordered 5 Div to hold on until they considered it would be dangerous to hold on any longer, in which case 3 Div would conform and 4 Div would cover the operation.

At 2 pm orders were given to 5 Div to withdraw their artillery. The CRA 5 Div accordingly sent Major Tailyour, his brigade-major, to collect the gun teams and arrange the withdrawal. Colonel Stevens refused to leave whilst any of his guns were still in action and both he and Major Tailyour were later taken prisoner.

It was decided not to attempt the withdrawal of 52 Battery as it was now in such an exposed position and so many of its horses had been destroyed. The remaining teams of 52 Battery were to be used to assist in recovering 37 Battery and 80 Battery. The remaining guns of 52 Battery continued firing until the end. All of 11 Battery's guns had been silenced. All the officers had been hit and Sergeant Hopper was the senior survivor. 11 Battery's teams were the first up. One team was knocked out on the way but five guns were limbered up and driven off, taking the wounded battery commander, Major Henning, on a limber; but this was overturned in a sunken road. Henning, however, was picked up later by 80 Battery. He was awarded the DSO. Major Birley, commanding 80 Battery, despite being heavily shelled, got five of his guns away, the wounded being carried on the limbers. Birley was hit twice more on the way back.

These daring attempts to withdraw the guns, which the Germans must have thought impossible, were surprisingly successful; four guns of 11 Battery, five of 80 Battery and four howitzers of 37 Battery were driven away and saved. Nevertheless two gun teams were blown to pieces on the way up and it was only after great efforts that the guns were extricated. The survivors of the batteries now disabled the remaining guns and themselves withdrew, carrying as many as possible of the wounded with them. And it was indeed high time that they retired as the German infantry were closing inexorably round the flank of the 2nd Suffolk Regiment and the machine-gun bullets were coming through the gun shields.

The Germans were now determined to assault, and masses of their infantry suddenly appeared out of the sunken road behind the line held by the 2nd Suffolks. The occupants of these trenches, a mixed lot consisting of men of the 2nd Suffolks, the 2nd Argyll and Sutherland Highlanders, and the 1st Dorset Regiment and RFA, opened rapid fire on the advancing German infantry and did so much execution that the Germans were temporarily halted.

Seeing that two abandoned howitzers of 37 Battery must fall into enemy hands, Captain Douglas Reynolds of the battery obtained permission from the CRA, who was on the spot, to call for volunteers to rescue them. Accompanied by Lieutenants E. C. Earle and W. D. Morgan, both of 37 Battery, Captain Reynolds led up two teams to bring out the guns. Despite the fact that the German infantry were only 100yd away they managed to limber up the two guns. But one entire team was immediately shot down and Driver Godley, the driver of the central pair of the other team, was killed. Reynolds, however, kept the remainder in hand and, with the assistance of Drivers Luke and Drain, brought one of the guns safely away. Captain Reynolds and Drivers Luke and Drain were awarded the Victoria Cross; Lieutenant Earle, who was wounded, received the DSO, and the sergeant and trumpeter the DCM. Earle was found stumbling along with a badly broken arm. He was hoisted on to a horse which was then hit. Later he was put on the back of a Clydesdale of the Heavy Battery. At the aid post at Beaumont Church he got a lift in an ambulance and escaped. Nearly all the wounded who had been taken to the church were captured.

Immediately afterwards, at 2.45 pm, a mass of German infantry swept over the doomed right flank and the 2nd Suffolk Regiment was overwhelmed, together with the men of the Manchesters, the Argylls and 15 Brigade RFA, who were with them.

52 Battery fought to the last gun and the last round. Three wounded sergeants remained working the guns to the end. They were all taken prisoner. In 15 Brigade, out of eighteen officers only four remained unwounded. The command of 15 Brigade devolved on Captain Higgon of 80 Battery. DSOs were awarded to Colonel Stevens and Majors Nutt, Henning and Birley, as well as to Major Jones of 37 Battery. Out of 23 officers the group had lost 16—about 70 per cent.

By 5 pm the whole of 2 Corps began its retreat with the rear-guards all in position. By 6 pm a drizzling rain had set in and the light had begun to fail. The enemy's pursuit died away. There was, of course, considerable confusion and congestion on the roads, with infantry, guns, transport and ambulances all converging on to them in no particular order. But the men marched on steadily and in silence. They were dead tired and very hungry but, rightly, very proud of themselves. Smith-Dorrien, who towards evening watched the 5th Division pass along the road south of Maurois, likened them to a crowd coming away from a race meeting—men smoking their pipes apparently quite unconcerned, walking steadily down the road.

Out of the 50,000 men engaged at Le Cateau, the total loss did not exceed 8,000. On 26 August 1914 the most powerful and best-equipped military machine the world had ever seen had been held in a bitter encounter by a British force much less than half its strength. At the end of the day the attackers had been so mauled that the pursuit of the German Army entirely changed its character. It ceased to be a reckless, thrusting, triumphant force and became much more respectful and hesitant. In fact, at Le Cateau, Smith-Dorrien, entirely on his own, took a big decision and did just what he said he was going to do; he 'gave the Germans a bloody nose', and then broke off the engagement and continued his withdrawal.

The *Official History* (*Military Operations France and Belgium 1914*, compiled by Brigadier-General Sir James Edmonds) has this to say:

German shells as we have seen followed the British as long as they were within sight and range and caused a few casualties, though not many; their guns also bombarded the evacuated positions with great fury until dark; but the cavalry and infantry made no attempt to press on. In fact, Smith-Dorrien's troops had done what GHQ feared was impossible. With both flanks more or less in the air, they had turned upon an enemy of at least twice their strength; had struck him hard, and had withdrawn, except on the right front of the 5th Division, practically without interference, with neither flank enveloped, having suffered losses severe, but, considering the circumstances, by no means extravagant. The men, after their magnificent rifle-shooting, looked upon themselves as victors; some indeed doubted whether they had been in a serious action. Yet they had inflicted upon the enemy casualties never revealed, which are believed to have been out of all proportion to their own;

and they had completely foiled the plan of the German commander and of OHL [Oberste Heeresleitung—German Supreme Command].

If ever there was an engagement where leadership counted, it was the battle of Le Cateau. And the leadership started from the top with the corps commander, General Sir Horace Smith-Dorrien. Had he not made his decision, which was an extremely courageous one—because his orders from Sir John French were to continue the withdrawal with all possible speed—the situation of the BEF might have been perilous indeed. Truly 'the law was in the circumstances' and in Smith-Dorrien's opinion the particular circumstances demanded the action which he took. General Allenby, commanding the Cavalry Division, deserves praise too. He was not under Smith-Dorrien's command, but, realising that a critical situation was threatening, he agreed wholeheartedly to take Smith-Dorrien's orders.

As a result of Le Cateau, 2 Corps were not seriously troubled during the rest of the retreat except by mounted troops and mobile detachments who kept at a respectful distance. Sir John French in his despatch of 7 September 1914 wrote of Le Cateau:

> I cannot close this brief account of the glorious stand of the British troops without putting on record my deep appreciation of the valuable services rendered by General Sir Horace Smith-Dorrien. I say without hesitation that the saving of the left wing of the Army under my command on the morning of 26th August could never have been accomplished unless a commander of rare and unusual coolness, intrepidity and determination had been present to personally conduct the operation.

General Joffre, the French Commander-in-Chief, telegraphed to Sir John French thanking him in the warmest terms for 'the powerful effect that the battle had had on the security of the left flank of the French Army'.

On 11 January 1915 the two corps commanders, Smith-Dorrien and Haig, were both decorated with the Grand Croix d'Officier of the Legion of Honour by the French President, Monsieur Poincaré. Yet three months later Sir John French summarily dismissed Smith-Dorrien from his Army command, at one day's notice, and sent him home.

General 'Wully' Robertson, Quarter-Master General to the BEF, who was a great friend and admirer of Smith-Dorrien, decided to break the news to the latter himself before he received the dismissal signal from the Adjutant-General. The story which had long been current in the Army and was confirmed later by Colonel Lord Malise Graham, then acting as ADC to Lieut-General Sir C. Ferguson, commanding 2 Corps, who was a spectator of the incident, was that Robertson drove up in his car somewhere in front of the Ypres salient, took Smith-Dorrien aside and remarked loudly enough for everyone present to hear: ' 'Orace, you're for 'ome.' And home Smith-Dorrien went. (Victor Bonham-Carter, *Soldier True.*)

Robertson put his dismissal down to French's rankling resentment over Le Cateau when, contrary to his orders, Smith-Dorrien had conducted such a successful and historic delaying action. Whatever the reason may have been, nothing can take from Smith-Dorrien the glory that was his.

That's what leadership means.

Robertson's opinion is entirely confirmed by the entry in Sir Douglas Haig's diary of 30 April 1915 when he records that Sir John French had visited him that day and said that he should have had Smith-Dorrien tried by court-martial because 'he had ordered him to retire from Le Cateau at 8 a.m., and he did not attempt to do so, but insisted on fighting on in spite of his orders to retire'. Although Sir John French had been compelled in his despatch of 7 September 1914 to acknowledge the great service Smith-Dorrien had rendered at Le Cateau, the fact that he had stolen his thunder rankled.

Generals can be very vindictive and there is no greater autocrat than an army commander in the field. He can sack anyone he likes—or dislikes—and there is no redress.

CHAPTER THREE

General Joffre and the Early French Disasters; the First Battle of Ypres

Winston Churchill writes in his *World Crisis*, Vol III, of

the immense miscalculations and almost fatal errors made by General Joffre in the first great collision of the war. The easterly and north-easterly attacks into which his four armies of the right and centre were impetuously launched were immediately stopped and hurled back with a slaughter so frightful that it has never yet been comprehended by the world.

The French infantry marched into battle conspicuous on the landscape in their red breeches and blue coats. The doctrine of the offensive, raised to the height of a religious frenzy, animated all ranks, and in no rank was it restrained by any foreknowledge of the power of magazine rifles and machine guns. A cruel shock lay before them. Everywhere along the battle front, whenever Germans were seen, the signal was given to charge. 'Vive la France, à la baionette—en avant', and the brave troops, nobly led by their regimental officers, responded in all the magnificent fighting fury for which the French nation has been traditionally renowned. In the mighty battle of the frontiers in the first few weeks of the war more than 300,000 Frenchmen were killed, wounded or made prisoners. However, General Joffre preserved his sangfroid amid these disastrous surprises to an extent which critics have declared almost indistinguishable from insensibility.

In all fairness to Joffre, it must be said that he had no responsibility for the French plan of all-out attack. But it is difficult to understand how he came to be appointed to a command of such great responsibility. He was a solid, well-balanced general, but he had never commanded a corps or an army. Indeed, he himself received the news of his high appointment with considerable embarrassment and misgiving. However, he certainly had the temperament and the physique to stand the strains which were put upon him. Actually, in the first three months of the war the French had lost in killed, wounded and prisoners, 854,000 men. In the same period the small British Army had lost 85,000, making a total Allied loss of 939,000.

Against this, in the same period, the Germans lost 677,000. But more than four-fifths of the French losses were sustained in the first shock. Had these gallant but impetuous French troops been handled with reason and prudence the course of the war might have taken a different turn. As it was the French Army really never recovered from the terrible wounds it suffered in the first few weeks—particularly as they were France's *corps d'élite*.

In September 1914 came the end of the retreat from Mons and the Allied offensives of the Marne and the Aisne. When the Aisne battle subsided into trench warfare in the second half of September the whole battlefront from the Swiss frontier to the Oise became stabilised. North of the Oise stretched 170km of empty space as far as the English Channel at Dunkirk. This area still allowed some liberty of manoeuvre and there then ensued a race to the sea on the part of both sides. Towards the end of September Sir John French suggested to Joffre that the BEF should be transferred from the Aisne front, where it was sandwiched between the French armies, to its original position on the extreme left of the French line. Joffre immediately concurred—particularly as further British troops were shortly to be landed on the coast of Flanders in an attempt to relieve the beleaguered fortress of Antwerp.

It was obviously desirable that all British forces should be concentrated in one sector of the front. The move from the Aisne front began on 2 October. 2 Corps moved to the Bethune area south-west of Lille, and on 19 October Haig's 1 Corps moved to Ypres. Meanwhile Antwerp had capitulated, the British Naval Division and the Belgian Field Army succeeding in extricating themselves just in time. On 7 October the newly formed British 7th Division disembarked at Zeebrugge and reached the neighbourhood of Ypres on the 14th. They joined the new 4 Corps under the command of General Sir Henry Rawlinson.

General Rawlinson had had a distinguished record and was to become one of the outstanding battle leaders in the First World War. He was born on 20 February 1864, the eldest son of Sir Henry Rawlinson, who was a distinguished administrative officer in the Middle East and India and also became a Member of Parliament. The young Henry was educated at Eton and Sandhurst and, on 20 February 1884, was commissioned in the 60th King's Royal Rifles and joined the 4th Battalion at Ferozepore in India. He was slim and wiry, good at games and fond of sport. He was particularly good at polo, a game which demands both skill and nerve. From the word go he was keen to master every detail of his profession and to become as distinguished as his father. Some people are born with the quality of leadership in them, others manage to acquire it by application and study. Rawlinson belonged to both categories. He soon gained experience of active service on the Indian frontier, which was a training-ground for so many prominent soldiers.

Rawlinson's first stroke of luck came when Sir Frederick Roberts (later Lord Roberts), who had just become commander-in-chief in India, invited him to come as an extra ADC for a big camp of exercise to be held in Delhi in the winter of 1885–6. Rawlinson did his job well and also distinguished himself by becoming a member of the Commander-in-Chief's polo team, which won the tournament held at the end of the manoeuvres. It was Lord Roberts's practice to select young officers of promise, test them thoroughly and, if they made good, to further their advancement. In November 1891, having been promoted captain

and obtained a transfer to the Coldstream Guards, Henry
Rawlinson passed into the Staff College. He was twenty-seven.
Amongst his fellow students were Byng, who was later to become
an army commander in France, and Henry Wilson, who was his
closest friend and a future field-marshal.

In 1898 Rawlinson was fortunate enough to be appointed to
the staff of Sir Herbert Kitchener, the Sirdar of the Egyptian
Army at the time of the Sudan campaign. He gave his first
impression of Kitchener:

> He is a curious and very strong character. I both like and admire
> him but on some minor points he is as obstinate as a com-
> missariat mule. He is a long-headed, clear-minded man of
> business with a wonderful memory. His apparent hardness of
> nature is a good deal put on and is I think due to a sort of
> shyness. It made him unpopular at first, but since those under
> him have come to realise what a thoroughly capable man he is
> there is a great deal less growling than there used to be.
>
> (Major-General Sir Frederick Maurice,
> *The Life of Lord Rawlinson of Trent*)

At the historic battle of Omdurman, Rawlinson was employed
by Kitchener in taking verbal orders to various commanders in
the field. Kitchener rarely issued a written order and yet kept
the details of each order in his head. When the dervishes advanced
in their masses Rawlinson was sent to order Captain (later Field-
Marshal) Douglas Haig, 7th Hussars, attached to the Egyptian
Army, gradually to withdraw his cavalry contact squadrons to
draw the enemy on.

In 1899 Rawlinson managed to get himself a staff appointment
on General Sir George White's staff at the start of the Boer War.
He went through the siege of Ladysmith and then, when Lord
Roberts arrived as commander-in-chief in 1901, he was sum-
moned to the latter's staff for the rest of the war. It was again
Lord Roberts who extricated him from a dull and uncongenial
job at the War Office to be Commandant at the Staff College
Camberley, which was of course one of the plum jobs in the Army

and very much after Henry Rawlinson's heart. He was the ideal man to give the College the fillip it needed in the general desire for a more professional and up-to-date image at that particular time. Rawlinson was only forty when he took over his Camberley duties. He had great panache, an attractive personality, a debonair spirit, high social standing and plenty of money.

To start with, Rawlinson did away with all examinations, with the exception of the entrance examination, and relied instead on the close personal acquaintance of himself and his directing staff with the students in assessing their capabilities. He initiated the study of combined naval and military operations with the Naval War College—which have been an important part of the curriculum at Camberley ever since, and subsequently with the RAF Staff College also.

Rawlinson was then appointed to the command of the 2nd Infantry Brigade at Aldershot and handed over charge of the Staff College to his friend, Henry Wilson, who was one of the most brilliant staff officers—though not commanders—of the First World War. Henry Wilson was a dynamic and inspiring personality. He was a great admirer of the French Army and he established a close liaison with General Foch, who was Commandant of the École Superieure in Paris. It was their collaboration that produced the plans governing the role of the BEF at the outbreak of war.

Wilson was succeeded as Commandant of the Staff College in 1910 by 'Wully' Robertson, one of the most remarkable soldiers in our history. He was the first ranker officer ever to become a field-marshal and a student at the Staff College—let alone its Commandant. At the Staff College Robertson made a lasting impression. He was a man who detested vague and high-sounding phrases. He epitomised in his teaching Foch's famous dictum: 'De quoi s'agit-il?', or, in common parlance, 'What is the problem?' And he always insisted that the students should be quite clear as to what the problem was before they began to think out its solution. He was also insistent that, although the Field Service Regulations laid stress on the offensive, the students should also study the defensive and even the retreat. He then went on to be

Director of Military Training at the War Office and Chief of Staff to Sir John French in 1915, and rose to be Chief of the Imperial General Staff. This was the pinnacle of his career. For two years of appalling responsibility and strain he moulded the strategy and organisation of the British Forces on all fronts. But in February 1918 his disagreement with Lloyd George led to his dismissal from the high office of CIGS, and he retired from the Army in 1920 with the rank of field-marshal.

But to return to the Western Front. During the latter part of October 1914 Haig's and Rawlinson's corps became more and more heavily engaged and it was evident that the Germans were intent on a major offensive to break through the British defence lines at Ypres.

At daybreak on 29 October the storm burst and Haig's 1 Corps was deluged with shells, followed by a heavy and ferocious infantry attack. Saturday, 31 October, was one of the most critical days in the history of the British Expeditionary Force and indeed of the British Empire. Urged on by the Kaiser himself, thirteen German battalions, shouting and cheering, succeeded in capturing the key point of Gheluvelt, near the junction of Haig's 1st and 7th Divisions. General Lomax, commanding the 1st Division, who had put in all his reserves, asked General Monro, who was commanding the 2nd Division on his left, for assistance and Monro sent him the 2nd Battalion of the Worcestershire Regiment. This battalion was put under the orders of the 1st (Guards) Brigade, commanded by Brigadier-General Fitzclarence.

Meanwhile a tragic disaster had struck, removing from the scene a number of valuable commanders and staff officers. General Lomax was holding a conference at his battle HQ at Hooge Château on the Menin Road, which was also attended by General Monro and some of his staff. At 1.15 pm the conference room was shattered by a salvo of four heavy shells. Lomax was mortally wounded and six of the staff officers were killed outright; Monro was only stunned; his ADC, Captain (later Field-Marshal) Gort, was not hurt. Shortly after this catastrophe Sir John French came up to Haig's command post and learnt of the gravity of the situation. The C-in-C was on the point of going

Page 51 (above left) General Sir Henry Rawlinson, perhaps the brainiest commander of them all; (above right) 2nd Lieut Harold Woolley, VC, 9th Battalion London Regiment, Hill 60 1915; (below) Admiral de Roebeck and General Sir Ian Hamilton (Commander-in-Chief in Gallipoli)

Page 52 (above left) Captain B. C. Freyberg, VC, commanding Hood Battalion RN Division, France 1916; (above right) Lieut A. Ball, VC, Royal Flying Corps, France, 1917; (below left) Winston Churchill, Secretary of State for War, with General Sir Henry Wilson; (below right) Lieut Augustus Agar, VC, who sank the Bolshevik Armoured Cruiser *Oleg* in Kronstadt Harbour on 17 June 1919

back to Cassel to tell Foch that the British line was broken and he must send up reinforcements urgently, when news arrived that the 2nd Worcesters had restored the situation by re-taking Gheluvelt.

This was a fantastic performance and was due, first and foremost to the inspired leadership of Major Edward Hankey, who had only just got command of the battalion. He decided that there was only one way to attack Gheluvelt and that was to surprise the enemy by getting up as close as possible to the German line and then to cover the open ground as quickly as possible in one single rush.

As the Worcesters breasted the Polderhoek Ridge and came in sight of Gheluvelt Château the German artillery got on to them and the battalion lost 100 men. But there was no stopping the gallant Worcesters and before the defenders from the 16th Bavarian Reserve Regiment had really tumbled to what was happening the Worcesters were in to them with the bayonet.

Major Hankey, a keen fox-hunting man, invariably carried a hunting horn to rally his men.* Many officers and men were decorated for their part in this splendid operation. Seldom in our history has the action of one battalion turned the tide of a critical situation in a major operation. And the result of their heroism was that other units, who had almost begun to assume that the war was lost, not only stood fast but counter-attacked in their turn.

The moment when Haig first heard that Gheluvelt was lost and that his corps's front was broken was one of the gravest of his career. His coolness in this great crisis was commended by all and added greatly to his reputation. He merely indicated on the map to his chief of staff the line on which his corps, if driven back from Ypres, must stand and fight to the last man. And then he took his usual afternoon ride, with his personal staff and cavalry outriders, slowly up the Menin road, back into the shelled area.

But as October gave way to November in conditions of icy

* My eldest son, John, who was killed on 7 May 1944 leading his company of the Queen's Royal Regiment at the battle of Kohima, also carried a hunting horn and was known as 'Hunting Horn Smyth'.

D

rain, sleet and swirling snow, there was no diminution of the German attacks. Then the Kaiser, who had come forward to the German Army Commander's advanced headquarters to urge his troops on, played his ace card—the famous Prussian Guard. Their orders were to take Ypres at all costs. They went forward fearlessly to conquer or to die; and they died—from the deluge of rapid Lee-Enfield rifle fire that the British infantry loosed upon them.

Finally, on 11 November the German artillery opened the most intense bombardment the British had ever experienced and then the infantry of ten German corps attacked the Ypres salient from every direction. The fiercest onslaught fell on Haig's front and particularly on the sector astride the Menin road, held by Fitzclarence's 1st (Guards) Brigade. North of the Menin road the enemy penetrated the British front to a depth of 500yd, but at the cost of very heavy casualties. Owing to Haig's foresight a number of strong points had been dug, and wired in, behind the forward defences and all brigade and battalion command posts were also prepared for defence.

By that evening Haig had put in every reserve he had. The gallant Brigadier-General Fitzclarence, who had performed prodigies of valour, led a desperate counter-attack by the Grenadiers and Irish Guards and fell, mortally wounded. But the British defence line held. On 12 November Haig's 1st Division could muster only 68 officers and 2,776 other ranks out of its nominal establishment of 18,000 and 1 Corps had lost more than half of its original effectives.

But the brunt of the German attack had been broken and by 20 November it petered out altogether. The first-line British infantry started cheering, a sound which spread along the whole battlefront.

CHAPTER FOUR

The Battle of Neuve Chapelle, the First Offensive from Trench Warfare Conditions

Neuve Chapelle was the first of the battles to be fought on the Western Front after the armies had settled down into conditions of continuous lines of trench systems, protected by fields of barbed wire and flanked by deadly concealed machine-gun nests, which together caused such a bloodbath in so many offensive operations. The queen of the defensive battle was undoubtedly the Vickers machine-gun.

This battle of Neuve Chapelle will be described in considerable detail because it not only formed a pattern for other trench warfare attacks but showed what a challenge to the generals, both senior and junior, this very novel form of warfare imposed. Leadership, above a battalion command, had never been more difficult—and was never to be so again.

Despite all the theories of postwar writers and critics there was only one way of conducting a major offensive operation on the Western Front and that was by breaking through the forward trench system and then exploiting success through the gap which had been created. But most of the attacks broke down at the first obstacle, or suffered such heavy casualties in surmounting it that they were unable to maintain the momentum and were easily pushed back by the fresh reserve formations of the defence.

The methods of making the breakthrough were strictly limited. Apart from the introduction of a new weapon, such as poison gas and the tank, the only way was by bringing to bear on the enemy wire and trenches such a massive weight of artillery fire that the wire was cut and the defenders' forward defences so shattered that the attacking waves of troops could capture them and then exploit the breakthrough.

The premier attacking arm, therefore, was the artillery, lots of it and large quantities of shells, which had to be dumped beforehand. As the war progressed and ever-increasing concentrations and barrages were demanded of the artillery the output of shells fell far below requirements. This shell shortage became a big political scandal and great efforts had to be made to overcome it. There were all sorts of factors which contributed to the attack's success or failure. If the preliminary artillery bombardment was too long, all surprise was lost. If it was too short, it might not achieve the object of cutting the wire and reducing the power of the defence. On so many occasions just one uncut field of barbed wire and one untouched machine-gun nest meant failure of the whole attack, with horrible slaughter. A heavy artillery bombardment had its disadvantages for the attacker. It cut up the ground and made movement slow, and it made communications and visibility difficult. The infantry attack plan had to be worked out in strict and minute detail to conform with the artillery plan. This had to be prepared beforehand on a meticulous timetable which could not be altered once the whole operation had started. Then there was the factor of surprise, which was always most difficult to achieve in this type of warfare. And above all else there was the human factor. What was the infantryman to carry when he went into action? How soon could rations and ammunition be got up to him? If he carried everything he could possibly need he would look like a human pack-horse—and he wouldn't be able to fight. If he went into action too light he might run out of food and ammunition. Finally there was the all-important matter of the morale and fighting spirit of the troops and the drive and ability of the junior leaders, on whom so much depended.

The battle of Neuve Chapelle lasted three days, 10–13 March, and was carried out by the troops of the 1st Army under Haig. In January of that year General Sir William Robertson had become Chief of the General Staff to the British Expeditionary Force. Haig had the highest opinion of him and they worked in the closest harmony for the next three years, which was a great strength to the Army as a whole.

The system of attack which Haig adopted at Neuve Chapelle was one that he used in later battles, of course with adaptations to meet the particular conditions existing. It was carefully thought out and most thoroughly prepared. With conditions as they were at the time, the troops and artillery he had at his disposal, and what he knew of the German positions and strength, it would be difficult to fault his planning and his leadership. Although the amount of ground finally captured was negligible and the casualties heavy, Neuve Chapelle was definitely a morale-raiser for the British and for their Allies. The troops of Haig's Army showed that, in the unpromising conditions of trench warfare, the BEF could act effectively in attack just as it had done in the earlier withdrawals and defensive engagements.

Haig had asked Sir John French for at least another corps for this battle and as many heavy guns and howitzers as possible. He was given one extra division, the Canadian, and he had a total of 372 guns and 48 infantry battalions for his attack. Sir John French decided to retain at his own disposal the Cavalry Corps, the Indian Cavalry Corps and the 16th (North Midland) Division. Both French and Haig were cavalry soldiers and, just as their successors did in the Second World War, they liked to have some mobile troops ready to exploit success if an opportunity offered— the important difference being that horseflesh was more vulnerable to bullets and high explosives than armoured vehicles, and the latter could get through where horses couldn't.

By the middle of February Sir John French had approved Haig's plan of attack, which was to be carried out as soon after 9 March as weather conditions permitted. The all-important factor was the state of the ground. With water 18in below the surface it was impossible to entrench new positions which might be captured. It was therefore of the first importance that the attack should not be launched until the ground had dried.

With regard to the German opposition expected, it was known

that they had made considerable reductions in their strength for the operations in Russia and, as it turned out, only one German army corps of two divisions lay opposite the six divisions of the 1st Army on the narrow thirteen-mile frontage of attack between the La Bassée canal and Bois Grenier. It was possible for the Germans to bring in reinforcements from other parts of their line, but this would take time and it was estimated that it would take them about two days to bring in troops amounting to one division. In the event the Germans reinforced their battered front-line trench system remarkably quickly.

Haig's attack plan had two objectives: the first was the capture of Neuve Chapelle, and the second the capture of the Aubers ridge, nearly two miles further on.

On 15 February Haig held a conference with his three corps commanders, Monro commanding 1 Corps, Rawlinson 4 Corps, and Sir James Willcocks the Indian Corps. Having explained his general idea he gave each corps its special task. 1 Corps, on the right, was to gain the Orchard near La Quinque Rue; the Indian Corps in the centre was to take the south end of Neuve Chapelle and then the Bois du Biez; and on the left, 4 Corps was to take the rest of Neuve Chapelle and then Aubers village. Haig's plan was that the capture of Neuve Chapelle should be the first objective. It formed a salient in the German defence line from which all through the winter they had been able to enfilade the British trenches on either flank. Until the Neuve Chapelle salient had been captured or neutralised an advance on either side of it would be difficult. Then every effort was to be made to enlarge the gap created in the enemy's front by attacking simultaneously to the left and right of it and progressing towards the line Herlies–Illies on the Aubers ridge, thereby threatening the enemy's communications between La Bassée and Lille.

Haig himself laid down several principles on which the attack was to be based. First and foremost he insisted that the infantry was to advance as quickly as possible to take the fullest advantage of the artillery bombardment. It was hoped that this would not only smash the wire and the forward trench system but demoralise the defenders, at least temporarily. They must not be given time to recover, or to bring up reserves and reinforcements. At this conference with his corps commanders Haig directed that particular attention should be given to the following points: the passage through the British wire; the placing of guns in position gradually and secretly; the unostentatious registration of targets; the arrangements for bringing up the attacking troops to the assembly positions; the importance of trying to locate enemy machine-guns; and many other such details.

The importance of making passageways through our own wire was apt to be under-estimated and it was by no means an easy problem, particularly when the fields of protective wire got thicker. It took time and it had to be done under cover of darkness. If it were done too soon and too obviously, all surprise was lost; on the other hand, if the passages were too few and too narrow there was a lot of bunching and, if enemy patrols and Verey lights spotted it, heavy casualties were inflicted before the advance proper had commenced. Later in the war, when attacking troops generally advanced across no-man's-land behind a 'creeping' barrage of shellfire, this problem was usually solved by the first wave of the attack getting out of their trenches beforehand and joining up in no-man's-land. This, of course, had to be done under cover of darkness for a first-light attack. It demanded a high state of training and junior leadership—and complete secrecy. If the preliminary forming up was spotted by the enemy, they might inflict such heavy casualties on the attackers that the attack would be doomed to failure before it had started.

With regard to the preliminary bombardment, there were a number of important points to be settled. Experiments with live shell were carried out in the back areas, but there were still differences of opinion on several matters. The first one was the cutting of the enemy wire, without which any attack was doomed to costly failure. And here the critics of the leadership of the generals of the First World War must realise that the best was sometimes the enemy of the good. There was much difference of opinion amongst experts as to the number of shells required to destroy a given length of the German position at Neuve Chapelle. Later in the war the wire was thicker and the trenches stronger, perhaps with underground dugouts and galleries. Then new estimates had to be made. There were also differences of opinion as to whether shrapnel or high-explosive shells were best for cutting. With the fuze in use at that time, the conclusion was that shrapnel was preferable, as it cut the wire clean off the posts and left it lying in small pieces, whereas HE left it broken but still an entanglement. It was at first estimated that a bombardment of nearly three hours would be necessary, with the artillery available, to make certain of destroying the German forward positions. This would, of course, have eliminated the element of surprise altogether. Finally, at a meeting of all the CRAs concerned, it was decided that a bombardment of thirty-five minutes would be sufficient, both for cutting the wire and for destroying the German trenches. Haig directed his corps commanders to consider and report to him their allotment of artillery for destroying the wire and trenches, protecting the flanks of the attack, forming a 'cushion' behind the enemy's front trench system to prevent reinforcements coming up and neutralising the enemy's artillery and machine-guns.

On 16 February Haig for the first time interviewed Major Trenchard (afterwards to become the famous Marshal of the RAF), who commanded the flying wing under his orders, and asked for his proposals with regard to the allotment of aeroplanes for reconnaissance and artillery observation. Trenchard was much impressed by Haig's understanding of the possibilities of aerial co-operation at a time when few of the senior commanders appreciated the potential of the young air service.

Henceforth, for Haig, each day was devoted to the task of preparation for the attack. There were continual conferences with corps commanders and many consultations with other important officers concerned in the planning of the battle. Every day Haig visited the officers upon whom the principal responsibility would rest and impressed on them above everything the importance of making it plain to each of their subordinates exactly what his own part was to be. Each evening he would enter in his diary the opinion he had formed of the character and capacity of the officers he had interviewed. It is true that he did not, in the fashion of General Montgomery in the Second World War, speak to groups of soldiers and tell them what the plan was. To start with, neither Haig nor any of his corps commanders was geared to this sort of procedure, any more than Alexander or Auchinleck were. And in that form of trench warfare there was so little a senior commander could tell them—except to follow the barrage, kill Germans when they got on to their objective, and then dig in and hold on. Haig showed himself to his troops and inspected reserve formations, when he always appeared serene, calm, collected and full of confidence. In a short time he had made himself a master of the requirements of the trench-warfare battle. And he left no stone unturned to see that every phase of the plan of attack was as perfect as it could possibly be. This was the sort of leadership that troops understand and appreciate.

The French Parliament was now pressing Joffre to stage some offensive operation. Sir John French was pressing Haig to get started; but the latter was quite firm that, owing to the water-logged state of the ground, 10 March was the earliest date on which he could launch his attack. So 10 March it was.

The plan had now crystallised in every detail. The bombardment was to begin at 7.30 am, an hour after sunrise, by which time it was considered that the final registration of targets would have been carried out and that there would be sufficient light for accurate observation. During the next thirty-five minutes of the bombardment passages were to be cut through the German wire by 18pdr batteries firing shrapnel, whilst the howitzer batteries demolished the German front and support trenches. At 8.05 am the artillery would lift on to Neuve Chapelle village and the strong-points to the north and south. At the same time the infantry were to move forward from their breastworks and trenches, cross the 200yd of no-man's-land and carry out the assault before the Germans could recover from the effects of the bombardment. Three infantry brigades (one from the Indian Corps and two from 4 Corps) were detailed for this first assault. They were, from right to left, the Garhwal Brigade, 25 Brigade and 23 Brigade. On reaching the German support trenches, some 200yd beyond the front trench system, the leading troops of these three brigades were to wait till the end of the thirty-minute bombardment of the village of Neuve Chapelle. Then, at 8.35 am, the attack against the village was to be launched. The occupation of this line, running from the German defences opposite the Port Arthur salient on the right, along the eastern edge of Neuve Chapelle village to the German defences about the Moated Grange on the left, would conclude the opening stage of the battle.

From this point onwards the intention was to widen the gap by pressure of reserve formations of the remainder of the Indian Corps and 4 Corps. At a time to be decided by mutual agreement between these two corps commanders, both corps (less the three original assaulting brigades) would advance on to their final objective, the Aubers ridge, where they were to establish their position. This second stage of the operation was to be supported by a further artillery bombardment, particularly on to various known strong-points. It was hoped that 1 Corps, covering the right flank of the Indian Corps, and the Canadian division covering the left flank of 4 Corps, while assisting the initial stage by fire, would be able to take advantage of any weakening of the enemy front by assuming a vigorous offensive. If this was successful there would be a general advance of the 1st Army on to the higher and drier ground of the Aubers ridge.

In the ten days before the battle started a number of preliminary moves had to be made to get the troops into their right positions. All these movements had to be carried out under cover of darkness. This was an entirely new form of warfare for all the troops taking part, and indeed it was a method which had not been catered for in any of the prewar training manuals. All credit is due to Haig and his corps commanders for recognising the fact and being able to adapt themselves and their subordinate commanders to these new methods and conditions.

The three infantry brigades detailed to carry out the assault were withdrawn into rest billets on 2 March. Here they rehearsed the first phase of the operation in every detail. The officers of the assaulting units also visited the front-line trenches to see the places of assembly and their lines of advance. It was found necessary to construct additional trenches and lines of breastworks—

forming-up trenches as close as possible to the front line. In the later stages of the war, when air photography had become a fine art, it would have have been so easy to conceal these. Advance dumps had to be established to contain rations, entrenching tools and engineer stores. Magazines were constructed for storing ammunition and bombs. Light tramlines made of wooden rails and sleepers (to deaden the noise) were laid to transport all these supplies up to positions close behind the front-line trenches.

All these preparations had to be greatly multiplied in later battles when more guns and more troops were used and they entailed far more intensified precautions to avoid all surprise being lost.

The Royal Flying Corps carried out reconnaissances and observations for the artillery on an unprecedented scale. It also photographed the enemy positions up to a depth of 1,500yd.

The three assaulting brigades had to be in position in the trenches and breastworks previously prepared for them by 4.30 am on 10 March. No unit had more than five miles to march and they were all given a hot meal beforehand. On the eve of the battle there had been rain and sleet, and in fact the weather conditions were so unpropitious that, at the last minute, serious consideration was given to postponing the attack for twenty-four hours. This would have entailed the attacking brigades having to remain all day in their forming-up trenches, which would not only have been very uncomfortable and morale-lowering, but also possibly very dangerous. However, at about 6.30 am the mist and clouds began to clear, and Haig, from his advanced headquarters at Merville, wisely ordered that the attack should be carried out as planned.

The bombardment of the enemy's trenches and strong-points, during which 3,000 shells were expended, was generally most effective, the German front-line trenches being practically obliterated with the exception of about 400yd on the front of 23 Brigade, which suffered very heavy casualties. The assault of the right battalion of the Garhwal Brigade, the 1/39th Garhwalis under Lieut-Colonel Swiney, met with misfortune almost immediately. They took a wrong direction in the early morning mist and attacked a portion of the German defences which had not been dealt with by the preliminary bombardment. Despite this, they forced their way most gallantly through the unbroken wire and captured 200yd of German trenches—but at terrible cost. All the six British officers leading the assault were killed and other officers were wounded. With no British officers left, the battalion held its ground—a splendid achievement. The attack of the other three battalions was more easily successful. They advanced quickly across no-man's-land, found the wire and trenches destroyed and occupied the German trenches with little opposition. They then passed straight on to the German support trench which they captured within fifteen minutes of the start of their advance. By 9 am they had reached their brigade objective and captured 200 prisoners and 5 machine-guns. They then set to work to entrench their position.

When our troops entered Neuve Chapelle on the morning of 10 March they found that the effect of our bombardment resembled that of a very violent earthquake. The church had been completely shattered and the churchyard was pitted from end to end with yawning shell-holes, the graves in many places being burst open and long-buried corpses strewn around to add to those of the German defenders. Many of the trees had been blown up at the roots and over all was the stain and pungent reek of lyddite. But the gallant German infantry and machine-gunners still hung on in the ruins, inflicting a number of casualties on our troops before they surrendered.

25 Brigade of the 8th Division (4 Corps), under Brigadier-General Lowry Cole, going into action for the first time in the war, on the left of the Garhwal Brigade, with the 2nd Royal Berkshire Regiment and the 2nd Lincolnshire Regiment leading, crossed no-man's-land with little loss. The Germans were quite unable to man their devastated trenches. The attacking battalions pushed straight on to the support trenches which they reached at 8.20 am. After the second phase of the bombardment had been completed at 8.33 am the 2nd Rifle Brigade and the 1st Royal Irish Rifles passed through the leading battalions and joined up with the Garhwal Brigade on the far side of Neuve Chapelle.

25 Brigade had reached their objective, capturing over fifty prisoners, and began to entrench their position.

On their left, however, 23 Brigade, commanded by Brigadier-General Pinney, had run into severe trouble owing to some of the German trenches not having been touched by the bombardment. The brigade had advanced with the 2nd Middlesex Regiment on the left, the 2nd Scottish Rifles on the right and the 2nd Devonshires in support, with the 2nd West Yorkshire in brigade reserve. It was the 200yd of German trench opposite the Middlesex Regiment which had been undamaged. The three leading waves of the Middlesex Regiment were completely annihilated by murderous rifle and machine-gun fire and the Germans in this sector then turned their attention to the 2nd Scottish Rifles, who also suffered very severely. They had only three officers left in action.

Apparently this very unfortunate artillery failure was due to two siege batteries which had arrived from the United Kingdom only the previous day and had not been able to register targets or lay out lines to their forward observing officers. Certainly Sir Douglas Haig and General Rawlinson could in no way be blamed for this ghastly error, which not only caused the unnecessary death of so many gallant officers and men, but entirely held up the whole advance which had made such a splendid start in other sectors.

In so many of the subsequent trench warfare offensives, which had to be so meticulously planned, quite a small error in the artillery plan, or failure to cut lanes through our own wire, or to flatten the enemy's, resulted in disaster in one particular sector of the attack. And this might enable the enemy holding that sector the bring enfilade fire against the sectors on either side of it.

Meanwhile the further attack of the Meerut Division had been held up by continued German resistance on the 1/39th Garhwali front, which was being cleared up by the 1st Seaforth Highlanders. It was not until mid-afternoon, therefore, that 4 Corps was ready to conform by advancing on the Bois du Biez. But these six or seven hours' delay in the momentum of the attack were to prove fatal to any considerable success.

The Germans recovered from their shattering early-morning

reverses with their usual speed and fanatical bravery and they made the fullest use of the respite which had been granted to them by establishing a new reserve position and strengthening the strong-points in their rear defences, which had not yet been attacked. Throughout 11 March the Indian Corps and 4 Corps were using their reserve formations to press forward towards the Bois du Biez and the Aubers ridge against stiffening German resistance. During the night of the 11/12th the Germans brought forward considerable reinforcements and before dawn on the 12th they counter-attacked fiercely along the whole front of the original British line, covered by a heavy artillery bombardment. This was not nearly so crushing or so accurate as the British opening bombardment on the morning of the 10th, as was only natural owing to the short time they had in which to prepare it. But it was quite heavy and was encouraging to the German infantry who moved forward under cover of a thick mist to within 60yd of the British position before they came into view. The German attack was repulsed everywhere with heavy losses. But the thick haze, combined with the fog of war, prevented information getting back which would have enabled an immediate British counter-attack to be staged and the Germans were given time to recover. These factors prevented the British artillery from registering on new targets.

When the counter-attacks went in on the fronts of both British corps, they met with hard fighting and varying success. Haig himself went forward to both corps headquarters to urge the continuance of the offensive. But, during the evening, reports received by Haig made it clear that the Germans had constructed a new position east of Neuve Chapelle which they were holding in strength, and resistance was stiffening all along the front. He therefore ordered that the positions gained should be wired and secured against attack. So this important battle of Neuve Chapelle had virtually come to an end on the night of 12 March. A local offensive was launched on the following morning by the 7th Division of 4 Corps to straighten out the line. This was defeated with heavy loss to the 6th Gordon Highlanders and 1st Grenadier Guards. It was this sort of operation, staged with inadequate artillery support, without any element of surprise whatsoever, and without any real tactical necessity, which was a negation of leadership and so much reduced the confidence of the PBI in their commanders.

During the 13th and 14th the new front lines of both sides were consolidated and reliefs were carried out under cover of darkness. The British casualties were 583 officers and 12,309 other ranks. The German casualties were probably much the same and included 30 officers and 1,657 other ranks taken prisoner. Neuve Chapelle was important in that it was the first planned trench battle that had been carried out in the war. As such it became a landmark and a basis for other battles. It indicated the problems of attack and defence, and how they could be met. It demonstrated the meticulous preparation that was necessary for success; the limitations imposed upon command and leadership when the battle had actually been launched; the difficulties of mutual support between infantry and artillery during the second phase, when the break-in had been achieved; the ever-present danger of wire and machine-gun nests that had escaped the bombardment; and the staunchness of so many German sub-units who fought it out to the end—all these could conspire to wreak havoc with the best-laid plans. All that old training of fire and movement had gone with the wind. The trench-warfare soldier was a different sort of animal. He lived underground in conditions of extreme boredom, punctuated by periods of extreme danger. And the snipers were always a menace—particularly to the officers upon whom they concentrated their attention. Then, just before a battle was coming up the soldier was 'fattened up' for it; he had to make himself 'word perfect' in the limited but vital things he had to do. And when the whistle blew for the 'off' he had to show fortitude and endurance beyond anything that had ever been dreamed of: and death and disablement followed him wherever he went.

Sir John French was critical of General Rawlinson in his despatch of 5 April 1915. He wrote:

I am of the opinion that this delay would not have occurred

had the clearly expressed order of the General Officer Commanding First Army been more carefully observed. The difficulties might have been overcome at an early period of the first day if the GOC 4 Corps had been able to bring his reserve brigade more readily into action.

(The Life of Lord Rawlinson of Trent)

This was not strictly correct, as is the case with so many higher commanders' despatches. The delay in 4 Corps was because the artillery plan for the initial bombardment had a big hole in it, which caused devastation to two of the front-line attacking battalions. And General Rawlinson also skated over this regrettable occurrence in his despatch.

However, Rawlinson in return had a dig at Sir John when he wrote on 25 March:

The losses are the feature most to be deplored. The great majority occurred on the second and third days, in attacking the enemy's pivots and houses. These losses might all have been avoided if we had been content with the capture of the village of Neuve Chapelle itself, instead of persisting in pressing on in order to get the cavalry through. I confess that this idea does not appeal to me. The cavalry will I fear do no good when they go through for they are certain to be held up by wire and trenches in whatever direction they may attempt to go. The enemy are not yet sufficiently demoralised to hunt them with cavalry. We must wait before that happy state of affairs supervenes. What we want to do now is what I call 'bite and hold'. Bite off a piece of the enemy's line like Neuve Chapelle and hold it against counter-attack. The bite can be made without much loss, and, if we choose the right place and make every preparation to put it quickly into a state of defence, there ought to be no difficulty in holding it against the enemy's counter-attacks, and in inflicting on him at least twice the loss that we have suffered in making the bite. This policy, I think, we should adopt all along the line.

There is a lot of very sound sense in what Sir Henry Rawlinson wrote, and in fact this policy of 'attack with a limited objective' was generally adopted on the Western Front some two-and-a-half years later. But Rawlinson was advocating it immediately after Neuve Chapelle was fought. Had the battle been fought on his way of thinking the Middlesex Regiment and the Scottish Rifles would still have suffered heavily in the first assault. Apart from that, we should have achieved by midday on the first day, with far fewer casualties, all the ground—and more—than what we did finally manage to hold; we should have had much more time to dig in and wire the new position; and when the German counter-attack came, as it inevitably would have done, we would have inflicted far heavier casualties on him because our new positions would have been so much stronger and there would have been time to arrange for far better artillery support. General Rawlinson was one of the best and wisest battle leaders of the First World War.

Nine VCs were awarded in the battle of Neuve Chapelle, between 10 and 12 March 1915. The first went to Rifleman Gobar Singh Negi of the 2nd Battalion 39th Garhwal Rifles who were in the leading wave of the attack. As soon as the artillery barrage lifted the battalion followed it at the double, taking the fullest possible advantage of the crushing effect of the shelling. The 2/39th pressed on, passed the first line of German trenches and took the second. During the assault on the main position Rifleman Gobar Singh Negi was one of the bayonet men accompanying a bombing party. He was the first man to go round every traverse, killing several of the enemy and forcing the remainder to surrender. He himself was killed afterwards and was awarded his Cross posthumously. Great courage was needed to be first round a traverse, not knowing what might be round the corner, and the first man faced the greatest danger of instant death. On the other hand, the sudden sight of a fierce-looking Indian wielding cold steel with dash and determination had a great effect on whoever was in the trench—and there were many instances of whole groups of Germans surrendering.

The other VC awarded on the first day of the battle was that

E

of Private William Buckingham, of the 2nd Battalion the Leicester Regiment, for conspicuous acts of bravery in rescuing wounded men under heavy fire. The seven other VCs were awarded on 12 March, the third day of the battle.

The action at Hill 60, two miles east of Ypres, on 20/21 April 1915 was one of the most heroic in the history of British arms and the very name 'Hill 60' became a household word in the Britain of the First World War. Hill 60 was really just a heap of earth, but it was important because it afforded an artillery observation post (AOP) from which a large portion of the front could be commanded. On 17 April the British had exploded several mines under the hill, after which, under cover of heavy artillery fire, it was stormed at the point of the bayonet. The enemy counter-attacked strongly and fierce hand-to-hand fighting took place, as a result of which the Germans regained most of the hill. The British, however, again took the hill in a bayonet assault. But the Germans returned to the attack and throughout the 19th and 20th the hill was subjected to a terrific artillery battering, followed by infantry and bombing attacks.

This epic struggle for ground, which was what so many 'dog-fights' in this period of the war on the Western Front were all about, won three VCs for the 1st Battalion East Surrey Regiment and one for the 9th Battalion London Regiment of the Territorial Force.

Lieutenant George Rowland Patrick Roupell had fought at Mons, Le Cateau, the Marne and the Aisne and at the first battle of Ypres. On 20 April 1915 he was commanding a company of his battalion in a front-line trench on Hill 60, which was subjected to a very severe bombardment throughout the day. Towards evening the bombardment intensified and strong German bombing parties worked their way along the communication trenches linking their front line with ours. Lieutenant Roupell, though wounded in several places, remained at his post and led his company in repelling a strong German assault. During a lull in the operations he had his wounds dressed and then insisted on returning to his trench. He held the position throughout the night and was one of the few survivors of his company when his battalion was relieved next morning. They don't come more gallant than George Roupell.

Second Lieutenant Geoffrey Harold Woolley was the son of a clergyman in East London. He went out to France with the 9th Battalion the London Regiment (Queen Victoria's Rifles) in November 1914 and they became the first unit in the Territorial Force to gain a VC. It happened like this. Two companies of the battalion had come to the rescue at a very critical time in the desperate struggle for Hill 60. Both the company commanders had been killed and two-thirds of the men had fallen. It was touch and go whether the survivors could stick it any longer. But the arrival of 2nd Lieutenant Woolley put new heart into them and saved the situation. Although Woolley remained the only officer on Hill 60 at the time, he successfully resisted all attacks on his position and continued throwing bombs and encouraging his men until he was relieved.

Four days after this epic fight at Hill 60 the first Canadian VC of the war was won by Captain Edward Donald Bellew of the 7th Canadian Infantry Battalion in the British Columbia Regiment. The incident occurred during the German attack on the Ypres Salient. Bellew, as battalion machine-gun officer, had two guns in action on the high ground overlooking Keerselaere when the enemy's attack broke in full force against the 7th Canadians. Reinforcements were sent forward, but they were surrounded and destroyed. The enemy were established in strength less than 100yd away; no further assistance was in sight, and the rear of the position was also threatened. Nevertheless Captain Bellew and Sergeant Peerless, each operating a gun, decided to stay where they were and fight it out. Sergeant Peerless was killed and Captain Bellew was wounded and fell. But he managed to get up and maintained his fire until his ammunition failed and the Germans rushed the position. Captain Bellew then seized a rifle, smashed his machine-gun, and, fighting to the last, was taken prisoner.

CHAPTER FIVE

Gallipoli: the Landings

Early in 1915 the British War Council, which had been formed
at the end of November 1914 to advise the Cabinet on the strategy
and direction of the war, gave its earnest consideration to a
memorandum by Lieut-Colonel Hankey, its very highly regarded
secretary. Hankey exercised the same behind-the-scenes influence
in the First World War as 'Pug' Ismay did in the Second. In
fact Hankey's was a much more trained and intellectual influence
than Ismay's, though the latter's contribution, on a more personal
level as between Churchill and the Chiefs of Staff, was perhaps
even more valuable.

Hankey maintained that, following the first battle of Ypres,
a deadlock had been reached in France and that, unless some new
tactics were tried or some new weapons invented, we should
continue to batter our heads against a brick wall at an enormous cost in casualties. He put forward a plan to attack Turkey
and bring in all the Balkan states against her. Sir John French,
however, refused to admit that the state of deadlock on the
Western Front need be permanent. He maintained that, with
more artillery ammunition, infantry attacks of wider scope on
the German line could achieve a breakthrough.

The War Council discussed these proposals and decided to
mount a naval attack on the Dardanelles in February 1915. It
soon became apparent, however, that naval action by itself

would be unlikely to achieve success and it was agreed that a substantial military force would also be needed. Lord Kitchener became convinced of this when, early in March, he received a report from General Sir William Birdwood, whom he had sent out to the Dardanelles. Birdwood, who was closely in Lord Kitchener's confidence, was quite emphatic that the Fleet would not get through on its own. And how right he was, though success was at one time so very close. The problem, then, was to find the troops for a combined operation.

The 29th Division, the last of the uncommitted British regular divisions, had only recently arrived in England from India. The French had promised a division, and there were two New Zealand and Australian divisions (the Anzac Corps—Australian and New Zealand Army Corps) in Egypt that could be made available. This would make up a force of some 70,000 men. On 9 March the Anzacs sailed to the Aegean from Egypt and the next day Lord Kitchener decided that the 29th Division should follow.

Despite Birdwood's report and what had already taken place in Gallipoli, it was still thought that the Navy might break through and they were preparing to make another attempt, on a larger scale, to do so. Admiral Carden had sent a cable to London on 2 March saying that he hoped to get through to Constantinople in about fourteen days. Kitchener now had to appoint a commander-in-chief for the Gallipoli military force. All the most highly rated commanders were already in France. Birdwood, in command of the Anzacs, had high hopes that he would be selected, and was very disappointed when he was not. Kitchener chose General Sir Ian Hamilton, who was at that time in command of the Central Force, which was responsible for the defence of the United Kingdom. He was sixty-two years of age but fit and active both physically and mentally and undoubtedly one of the most capable and battle-experienced generals in the British Army. Kitchener had always thought highly of him, as had Winston Churchill. Churchill, as First Lord of the Admiralty, was of course closely concerned in the Gallipoli venture and had been its strongest supporter.

Ian Hamilton had been educated at Cheam, Wellington and Sandhurst. Having been gazetted in the Suffolk Regiment he transferred to the Gordon Highlanders in 1875. He was one of the young men whom Lord Roberts had picked out for accelerated promotion. Hamilton had seen active service in the Sudan, Burma, India and South Africa. Between 1905 and 1914 his appointments had been GOC Southern Command, Adjutant-General to the Forces, and GOC Malta.

Hamilton was an unusual type of soldier, being not only a fine sportsman but a good painter, a lover of music and poetry and a fine writer. He had great personal charm, immense courage and daring and an excellent brain. He was not, however, a dynamic commander. His slight figure was curiously angular in appearance; his uniform never seemed to fit him and his service cap sat on his head like a pancake. If he had a fault as a leader in battle it was perhaps a lack of drive and ruthlessness.

Birdwood was always known as 'Birdie' and in the coming campaign as 'the Soul of Anzac'. He was an Indian Army officer of magnificent physique and presence and a leader of men to his finger-tips. Without the wide experience and intellectual powers of Ian Hamilton, he looked to be the leader he was. Small in stature, squarely built, determined, courageous and reliable, he was eminently sound in all his military thinking. There was nothing flamboyant about him but he was always well turned out. He was in many ways of the same type as Field-Marshal Lord Alexander in the Second World War. Both were fine athletes and kept themselves in tip-top physical condition. Birdwood was a teetotaller, a non-smoker and a very moderate eater.

Before starting on this fateful assignment, Ian Hamilton was given some brief instructions in writing. He was to await the Fleet's action in the Dardanelles on 18 March. If it was successful he was to hold the peninsula with a light garrison and advance direct upon Constantinople, where he might expect to be joined by a Russian corps which would be landed in the Bosphorus. In no circumstances was he to start operations until his whole force was assembled; and he was not to operate on the Adriatic side of the Dardanelles. Beyond this he was told practically nothing about the enemy, or the country. Even the maps and handbooks available were very scarce and completely out of date. A very scratch staff, few of whom he had ever seen before, were hastily assembled and the whole outfit set off from London on 13 March and arrived in the Dardanelles on the 17th. They were just in time to see the Navy's unsuccessful attempt to force the Narrows on 18 March, with the loss of several battleships. Two days earlier the naval commander-in-chief, Vice-Admiral Carden, had gone sick and the naval command had devolved upon his deputy, Vice-Admiral de Roebeck.

On 22 March Hamilton and de Roebeck decided that only a combined operation with naval and military forces could be successful in capturing the Gallipoli peninsula and commanding the Dardanelles. After many cables had passed between Gallipoli and Whitehall it was left to Hamilton and de Roebeck to decide between them what should be done and how the operations should be conducted. All the War Council decided was that the Greek island of Lemnos, with its large harbour of Mudros, big enough for a number of troopships, should be the base of operations. Kitchener left Hamilton in no doubt that speed was essential and that his assault on Gallipoli should take place not later than the middle of April.

It would be difficult to find any commander in our history who was saddled with a task as difficult and unpromising as that which faced Ian Hamilton at this time. An amphibious operation which entails landing troops on defended beaches is hazardous enough at any time. But when the all-important element of surprise has gone and the defenders know, within fairly narrow limits, where the attacks are likely to come, the whole operation presents almost insuperable difficulties.

The British force which had been assembling in Egypt was a very mixed bag indeed. There were the French, looking magnificent in their red breeches and blue coats—yet seeming to be attired for some other war which was dead and gone. There were Zouaves, Gurkhas from India, and Greeks. There were Scottish, English and Irish troops and sailors from the British and French navies. And there were the New Zealanders and the

Australians who became famous as the Anzacs. But at that time the 30,000 Anzacs, who comprised nearly half the infantry at Ian Hamilton's disposal, were an unknown quantity. They were all volunteers. Their discipline—and particularly their saluting—was more honoured in the breach than in the observance. But they were grand men, tall, lithe and strong—and as brave as they come. The 29th British Division, of some 17,000 men, all regulars from India and other overseas stations, was at this stage of the war—compared to the battle-worn British divisions in France—just about the finest fighting material we had.

Hamilton's 75,000 men had first to be transported from Egypt to Lemnos, a distance of 700 miles. The whole outfit, together with 1,600 horses, donkeys and mules and 300 vehicles, moved to Mudros harbour, which became crammed with shipping. There were battleships, colliers, destroyers, mine-sweepers, troop transports, hospital ships and all sorts of other craft. This was the biggest amphibious operation that had ever been staged. When one remembers the two years of preparation for the Normandy landing in 1944 it is quite fantastic that Hamilton's scratch force should have been expected to assemble in Egypt, move by sea to Lemnos and launch its assault on Gallipoli in a matter of a few weeks. Hamilton lacked a number of the essentials for such a difficult amphibious operation. He had a scratch headquarters staff, most of whom he didn't know, no up-to-date maps of the area, no intelligence organisation and very little knowledge of the numbers and dispositions of the Turks, and very little up-to-date signalling equipment. Also, although he had an efficient Fleet to co-operate with him, neither they nor his troops had had any combined training in the very difficult tasks which faced them, in which everything depended on their co-operating closely together—particularly with regard to communications. Also, of course, ships' guns, though powerful and frightening to an enemy on shore, are not the best weapons to give close support to attacking infantry. Their trajectory is so flat that they can't drop shells just over the hill and the Turks were able to take cover during the naval bombardments and then come forward and man their trenches when they had ceased.

The defence of the Gallipoli peninsula did not present any great problems to the Turks. An invading force would have to land on one or more of the beaches and then attempt to gain possession of the high ground which dominated the Dardanelles. They were really only four main beaches on the peninsula: Bulair at the neck; Suvla Bay half-way down; Ari Burnu and Gaba Tepe still further south; and those at the tip of Cape Helles. Behind all these landing-places there was high ground which formed a spine running all the way down the peninsula; but the really important eminences were the ridge which made a semi-circle around Suvla Bay, the Sari Bair chain just to the north of Ari Burnu, and Achi Baba, which was about five miles north of the Cape Helles beaches and dominated them entirely. Beaches also existed on the eastern side of the Dardanelles, but they would come under fire from Turkish guns on the Asiatic side. There was also the possibility that an invading enemy might come ashore somewhere on the Adriatic side.

Liman von Sanders had been appointed commander-in-chief of the Gallipoli forces by Enver Pasha, the Turkish Minister of Defence, in March 1915. Von Sanders had started his military service at the age of nineteen as an infantry officer in the Prussian Army. By 1911 he had risen to the rank of lieutenant-general. When Turkey came into the war he was given the task of re-organising and preparing the Army. He had appointed a number of German officers to important posts. Although a number of the Turkish officers did not like having these Germans, they did in fact provide that military expertise and professionalism which the Turkish Army needed.

Liman von Sanders had at his disposal for the defence of Gallipoli some 80,000 men, organised into six divisions. They had been dispersed round the peninsula and his first task was to concentrate them at the places where he thought the British were most likely to invade. It appeared to him that the point of most danger was the Asiatic shore and he accordingly placed two of his six divisions there. This appreciation by von Sanders is interesting because it was here that General Birdwood wanted the main landing to take place—but he was overruled. Liman

The landings at Gallipoli

von Sanders obviously agreed with Birdwood that this was the most dangerous course from the Turkish point of view. Kitchener had been undecided whether Birdwood or Hamilton should be appointed commander-in-chief in Gallipoli. Had he chosen Birdwood the Gallipoli campaign would have taken a very different course, for better or worse. But it could hardly have been worse.

Liman von Sanders regarded Bulair, at the northern neck of the Dardanelles, as next in priority, and here he placed two divisions. The British did make a diversion there but they considered it too risky to do more than that. His fifth division he sent to Cape Helles; and to the sixth division he gave a special role. It was to remain near Mudros in the Narrows as a general reserve, ready to go north to Bulair, south to Cape Helles, or across the Straits to Asia. He gave command of this division to a comparatively young Turkish officer, Mustapha Kemal, who was only thirty-four. The latter was a fanatically keen student of his profession, determined to make a name for himself, both as a soldier and as a politician. He was to play a decisive part in the Gallipoli campaign in halting and throwing back the Anzac landing at Ari Burnu. He was later given command of the 16th Turkish Army Corps.

As they had repulsed the British naval attack on 18 March, the morale of the Turkish defenders was naturally very high. Poorly equipped, poorly clothed and poorly paid, they yet showed immense courage and endurance and were really the 'surprise packet' for the British, particularly on the first day of the invasion. Liman von Sanders used the time the British had given him to good advantage. All the likely landing-places were protected by underwater wire and land mines. Roads were built across the hills to the peninsula, trenches were dug and artillery and small-arms training went on continuously.

Ian Hamilton quite realised that the most important military principle of surprise had been sacrificed and that nothing could now conceal from the Turks the fact that a large amphibious operation was impending; all he could hope to keep secret was where and when it would come. British reconnaissance planes were active but there was no doubt that Hamilton would have liked far more time

to prepare his attack. In fact, this question of haste, which Whitehall kept constantly urging, is difficult to understand. It is true
that all strategical surprise had been lost, but from the moment
the British force was concentrated in Lemnos tactical surprise
was on the side of the British. It was the Turks who now had to
dispose their forces in readiness for an attack in several possible
directions at any time. Theirs was now the tenseness and un-
certainty. The tactical initiative had passed to the British, who
could with advantage have taken another fortnight or three
weeks to gain more information, to perfect their inter-communica-
tion arrangements, to make some feints, perhaps to land some
small reconnaissance units and spy out the land.

One vital matter which, more than any other, caused the disastrous losses at the main landing-places was the underwater wire
which had been clearly disclosed by the aerial photographs. This
was a nightmare to Ian Hamilton which nagged at him all the
time and became a dreadful reality on 25 April as the unfortunate
landing troops became caught up in it. That was why he had
estimated 50 per cent casualties in the landings, and why General
Hunter-Weston, the commander of the 29th Division (undoubtedly
unwisely) said in a last-minute message to his troops: 'The eyes
of the world are on us. We must be prepared to face heavy losses
by bullets, shells, mines and drowning.' True, he didn't mention
wire—what would have been the point of doing so since nothing
was being done about it? The Navy (at home) was reputed to
have some new armoured invasion boats in course of preparation,
but they could be of no benefit now. It is difficult to understand
why naval torpedoes should not have been used to destroy some
of this underwater wire. It is true that the spread effect of a
torpedo is not great but the beaches were narrow. They would at
least have given some moral support to the attacking troops
and put a bit of wind up the Turks.

But time was pressing; the pundits in Whitehall were looking
at their watches and Ian Hamilton's deadline was almost past.
On 10 April he arrived in Mudros from Alexandria and held his
big planning conference with his leading naval and military
commanders. His plan, though necessarily complicated in its

details—as every combined operations plan is bound to be—was as simple as it could be in essentials. His main striking force was to be the 29th British Division. It was to go ashore on five small beaches (known as S, V, W, X and Y, from east to west) at Cape Helles at the extreme tip of the peninsula. It was hoped that, by the end of the first day, it would have captured the crest of Achi Baba, six miles inland. Meanwhile Birdwood with his Anzacs was to land thirteen miles up the coast at Gaba Tepe. Then, striking across the peninsula through the Sari Bair hills, he was to make for the heights of Mel Tepe. Thus the Turks opposing Hunter-Weston at Cape Helles would be cut off in the rear, and the hills dominating the Narrows would be in British hands.

Simultaneously two main diversions were to be carried out. The Royal Naval Division was to make a feint landing at Bulair and the French were to go ashore at Kum Kale on the Asiatic side of the Straits. Later these two forces would be brought back and put into the main attack. Admiral de Roebeck and his senior naval officers were delighted with the plan and it was generally agreed that, within the limits imposed by time and space, it was the best that could possibly have been devised. Both Birdwood and Hunter-Weston, who had had reservations and alternatives, appeared in the end to be persuaded that it was probably the best in the circumstances. But it differed in important essentials from the plan which Birdwood would have adopted had he been commander-in-chief.

It is, of course, easy to criticise after the event, but the fact remains that the main landings by the best-trained British force—the 29th Lancashire Division—were to be made on the beaches which were known to be most strongly defended and strongly wired. It is true that these were the easiest beaches for soldiers packed into small boats to land upon, and were the best for the subsequent landing of supplies and reinforcements. They were certainly the beaches on which the Turks expected us to land and for that reason alone were better avoided—anyway in the first landings. It would have been much better to have attempted to get far fewer troops ashore in the first landings at a number of points than to risk a big shambles at easier and more obvious landing-points.

Generally speaking, Ian Hamilton under-estimated the staunchness of the Turkish soldiery—as did Kitchener and the General Staff in London who gave Hamilton his orders. They all over-estimated the power of naval guns in an operation of this nature. Although strategical surprise had long since been lost there was still great scope for tactical surprise. More warships could well have been employed in the preliminary bombardment—some of them on beaches where no actual landing was going to take place. Above all, there was really no plan to use reserves to exploit success, partly because communications from ship to shore, and vice versa, were so bad. Most of these errors derived from the haste with which this very scratch force had to be committed to one of the most difficult amphibious operations in the history of warfare.

Whatever forebodings the higher command and staff had about the landings, the Fleet and the Army were in the highest spirits as D-Day approached. Mudros harbour, where some 200 ships were assembled, looked like a holiday regatta. Bands played on the ships, the men were cheering, and even the somewhat threatening weather conditions improved; by midnight on 24 April the sea had calmed and a bright moon shone over the surface of the Aegean.

While the Royal Naval Division steamed on throughout the night to launch their diversionary attack on Bulair, the Anzacs were transferred from their transports to the three battleships which were to take them to within a couple of miles of the shore. There, soon after 2 am on the morning of 25 April, they were transferred again to cutters which were taken in tow by pinnaces to within rowing distance of the beaches. The moon had now set and only faint starlight lit the sky.

The Anzac landings were made shortly before dawn with surprisingly little opposition. Then, suddenly, things began to go wrong. For some reason or other, whether from tides or eddies or navigational errors, the Gaba Tepe landing had been made at Ari Burnu, two miles further north. This surprised the Turks as much as it brought confusion to the Anzacs. The history books may say that this mistake was a great disaster: but if the Anzacs had landed, as they should have done, on the open beach of Gaba Tepe they would have been subjected to the murderous welcome given to the invaders on V and W beaches. As it was, the Anzacs came within an ace of winning the war—had it not been for Mustapha Kemal.

However, despite the confusion which ensued from having landed at the wrong place, some 15,000 Anzacs had been put ashore at Ari Burnu and had pushed forward over most difficult country against increasing Turkish opposition. In spite of this, they were still advancing. It was then that Mustapha Kemal realised that if the Anzacs captured Chunuk Bair and the Sari Bair ridge they would have established themselves on the commanding heights which dominated the Narrows and were really the key positions in this tense Gallipoli campaign. The Turks were on the retreat when Kemal came forward and at once realised the danger. He not only stopped the rot by his own forceful and courageous leadership, but ordered the whole of one Turkish regiment to counter-attack immediately and then requested permission to throw in the last regiment of his division as well.

Kemal then assumed command along the whole of the Anzac front. This inspired leadership on Kemal's part not only foiled and threw back the Anzac attack on Chunuk Bair but really decided the fate of the Gallipoli compaign. On such things does the difference between victory and defeat often depend. Afterwards the Turks acknowledged that if the Anzac landing had succeeded in capturing the commanding heights, which it so nearly did, it would have struck a fatal blow at the heart of the Turkish defences.

Meanwhile, some thirteen miles south at Cape Helles, the 29th Division, under General Hunter-Weston, were attempting to make their five separate landings around the toe of the peninsula. At Y beach, about four miles up the coast on the western side of the peninsula, 2,000 men were put ashore without a shot being fired at them. Their mission was to thrust inland and take the

Turkish defenders in the rear. This could perfectly well have been done—and could have had a decisive effect—but Hunter-Weston's verbal orders to the senior commanders at Y beach were so unclear that they just sat there and awaited further instructions. Indeed, it was not even clear which of two colonels on this landing was in charge.

At X beach, also just north of Tekke Burnu, two companies of the Royal Fusiliers had landed at 6.30 am without a single casualty and from the summit of the cliff they had occupied they could see right across the peninsula to S beach at Morto Bay, where the South Wales Borderers had easily overcome the light opposition they had met and were digging in.

Hunter-Weston must be severely criticised for the fact that, owing to the vagueness of his orders, the successful landings at X and Y beaches were not exploited vigorously and for the fact that he was so completely out of touch with these two landings. At the other landings, where severe opposition was experienced and there were heavy casualties, there was some excuse for no shore-to-ship signals being sent. But there was no excuse whatever in the case of completely unopposed landings. It is for this sort of reason that amphibious operations are lost or won.

It had been assumed that the main beaches, W and V, would be heavily defended, and Ian Hamilton's plan was that the defence should be destroyed by a heavy naval bombardment. The battle-ship *Albion* bombarded the beaches for a full hour. To the attackers and to those viewing from the ships it seemed that no living thing could have survived in the target area, nor could any obstacle remain. At W beach, the scene of the famous 'Lancashire Landing', the Turkish defenders were shaken and decimated but their trenches and machine-guns were cleverly sited in re-entrants on either side of the beach, where the flat-trajectory naval guns could not reach them. They were also encouraged to see that the thick wire entanglements, which ran underwater along the whole length of the beach, were untouched. The naval covering fire ceased in plenty of time to allow the Turks to man their forward positions.

This famous 'Lancashire Landing' at W beach must surely be

classed as one of the finest examples of leadership and courage in the history of the British Army. But to go back a little. At the outbreak of war the 1st Battalion Lancashire Fusiliers had been stationed at Karachi in India. When they disembarked at Avonmouth on 2 January 1915 their red uniforms created quite a sensation among a population which had seen nothing but khaki since the beginning of the war. After a short spell of leave they had embarked for Gallipoli on 16 March, their strength then being 27 officers and 1,002 other ranks. They had arrived at Mudros on 10 April, where they had some practice in embarking and disembarking from ship's boats. All they learnt from this was that it was a difficult business, even with the men lightly loaded and in a calm sea. Perhaps it was just as well that they didn't know then the whole horror of the ordeal awaiting them. Their first casualty was the commanding officer who developed heart trouble and had to be invalided. So their leader in this great adventure was Major H. O. Bishop, with Major W. B. Pearson as second-in-command.

W Beach, the objective allotted to the Lancashire Fusiliers, was described by General Sir Ian Hamilton in his despatches as follows:

W beach consists of a strip of deep, powdery sand, some 350 yards long and from fifteen to forty yards wide, situated immediately south of Tekke Burnu, where a small gully running down to the sea opens a break in the cliffs. On either flank of the beach the ground rises precipitately; but in the centre, a number of sand dunes afford a more gradual aspect to the ridge overlooking the sea. Much time and ingenuity had been employed by the Turks in turning this landing place into a death-trap. Close to the water's edge a broad wire entanglement extended the whole length of the shore, and a supplementary barbed wire net-work lay concealed under the surface of the sea in the shallows. Land mines and sea mines had been laid. The high ground overlooking the beach was strongly fortified with trenches to which the gully afforded a natural covered approach. A number of machine guns were

F

also cunningly tucked away into holes in the cliff so as to be immune from naval bombardment whilst they were converging their fire upon the wire entanglements.

On the evening of 24 April, when the transports steamed slowly out of Mudros harbour, the Lancashire Fusiliers embarked in the cruiser HMS *Euryalus*, with the exception of D Company which was in HMS *Implacable*. The plan of attack had been made known to all ranks and a message from the king was read out to them. The battalion had not been in action for half a century and there was a feeling of tension and expectancy among them. The men were roused before dawn and given a meal whilst the ships took up their action stations for the preliminary bombardment, in which some 300 guns took part. Then, at 4 am, the battalion transferred into the ship's cutters—in tows of six to each company. It was a tight fit to get them in with their 70lb of kit per man.

The young midshipmen in charge of the steamboats came alongside and took the tows in charge. At 5 am, when the boats were clear of the ships, the bombardment began. Then, at 6 am, the boats headed for the shore. When the tows neared the beach the steamboats cast off and the ship's boats were rowed in by the four naval ratings in each boat.

As the first boatloads of Fusiliers came within 100yd of the shore the Turks opened a murderous fire upon them. Those men who survived the first fusilade tumbled out of the boats into 4ft of water. Many were hit in the water and a number were drowned, pulled under by their heavy packs or caught in the wire. It was a bloody shambles of tortured flesh, the screams of the wounded rising above the noise of the bullets. Nevertheless, with their rifles soaked and amidst great confusion, some of the survivors began to scramble through the wire—which had been completely untouched by the bombardment. Somehow the remains of C Company, under Captain R. R. Willis, getting together in some sort of formation, began to scale the cliff on one side of the beach, which was their company objective.

Meanwhile D Company, under Major G. S. Adams, had altered

course and landed on the rocks to the left of the headland Tekke Burnu. They attacked and bayoneted the Turkish holders of the machine-gun nest which had been the main cause of the damage to the other companies. D Company were then able to enfilade the Turkish trenches facing W beach. This was great leadership on the part of Major Adams, the company commander.

But in the water behind the wire lay over 300 Fusiliers who were either dead or seriously wounded. In this actual landing operation 63 out of 80 naval ratings were killed or wounded, and 11 officers and 350 men of the Fusiliers had become casualties. On the extreme right the attack on Hill 138 by A and B companies had struggled forward, though shattered by a naval shell which fell short. By 7.15 am some sort of position had been established sufficient to protect the beach from armed fire. C Company also reached its objective, though with many casualties.

As the afternoon wore on and Turkish reinforcements were thrown in to the counter-attack, the Lancashire Fusiliers, and the Worcesters on their flank, were hard pressed to hold on to their positions. But they did hold on somehow and did not yield an inch of ground. With the brigadier wounded and the brigade-major killed and the impossibility of getting any orders through to the junior leaders, the section, platoon and company commanders had to act on their own initiative.

The 25th of April was certainly a great day in the history of the Lancashire Fusiliers but also a sad one as, at the end of the day, they could muster only 11 officers and 399 men fit for duty out of the 1,002 who had embarked when they left England. The Divisional Commander asked the CO to submit six names from the battalion for the Victoria Cross. After consultation with his officers and men he submitted the names of Captain R. R. Willis (C Company Commander), Captain C. Bromley, Lance-Corporal A. Richards, Sergeant F. E. Stubbs (posthumous), Lance-Corporal J. Grimshaw and Private W. Keneally (posthumous). All six received the VC. In winning 'six VCs before breakfast' the 1st Battalion Lancashire Fusiliers nearly equalled the record number of VCs awarded to one regiment in a single action (seven, awarded to the South Wales Borderers at Rorke's Drift).

Perhaps the outstanding character among these VCs was Captain Bromley, the Adjutant, whose inspired and indomitable leadership was instrumental in getting the remnants of the battalion on to their objectives. He was thirty-seven at the time, unusually old for a VC. Bromley was twice wounded shortly afterwards and given command of the battalion. He was then wounded again and sent back to hospital in Alexandria. He begged to be allowed to rejoin the battalion in Gallipoli and was sent back in the *Royal Edward*. She was torpedoed and Bromley went down with the ship. The Royal Navy also won six VCs on this historic 25 April.

Even more ghastly scenes of carnage were seen on V beach. An important part of the plan for this landing centred round the converted collier *River Clyde*, from whose belly a living freight of some 2,000 men was to be put ashore. Large holes had been cut in her sides and sloping gangways were constructed so that the troops could rush down them as soon as the ship had grounded. By this method it was hoped to empty the ship within a few minutes. Machine-guns were mounted behind sandbags in the bows to hold the enemy down whilst landing was taking place. Here the Turkish defences were somewhat different but no less effective than on W beach. It was considered, however, that these defences could be shattered by the same bombardment from HMS *Albion* as was shelling W beach. Again, after the hour's bombardment, it appeared that all resistance had been crushed. But the Turks had retired during the shelling and crept quietly back when it ceased. There were only three platoons of them and four machine-guns. They held their fire until the last moment and then, when the causeway of boats was linked from the *River Clyde* to the shore, they opened a murderous fire on the men of the Munsters, the Dublin Fusiliers and the Hampshire Regiment. The *River Clyde* became a shambles, yet more and more men ran down the gangways to their death. By 9.30 am, out of 1,500 men who had attempted to land, only 200 had succeeded and had reached cover.

No less than six VCs were gained at V beach. It had been a costly and disastrous day from which the expedition never really recovered—but at least the British had established themselves ashore in several places. On the Anzac front there was a chaotic situation as a result of which, towards nightfall, General Birdwood, at the urgent request of his divisional commanders, had actually asked to be allowed to re-embark his forces. But Ian Hamilton had replied that they must dig in and stick it out. This was a difficult but vital decision which Ian Hamilton had to make when roused from his bed in the middle of the night. Had he not decided as he did the Anzacs might have suffered a great disaster.

At Y beach, where the troops had been undisturbed all day, the Turks attacked strongly in the evening. By daybreak the British had suffered 700 casualties and lost their commander. A general evacuation began. The Turks also retired. So the re-embarkation was unopposed, as the landing had been. All along the front the Turks had suffered quite heavy casualties and were content to rest on their laurels, which were considerable. On the British side magnificent courage had been shown in face of a situation which would have discouraged the boldest. Now, exhausted and deflated, with a cold rain falling, they had a grim task—to evacuate all the wounded and to strengthen their positions with the Turks holding the dominating ground above them.

Throughout this first day of the landings the higher commanders got no information as to what was happening, nor could they contribute anything to the grim battles which they could only glimpse vaguely through their field-glasses from the decks of ships. In actual fact, had they gone ashore with the troops they would have been no better off because they would have become embroiled in one little part of the battle—even if they had remained alive. Senior commanders who did go ashore were killed or wounded. The ships stood idly by ready to use their guns to support the troops but not knowing how or where. A strong air force would have been invaluable—but it didn't exist at that time.

It was not an easy matter for Ian Hamilton and his two principal subordinates, Generals Birdwood and Hunter-Weston, to decide where they would make their headquarters for the landings. Obviously, for the second phase of the operation, the advance from the beach-heads to the commanding heights, the two latter generals at any rate would have set up their headquarters ashore. But for the first phase they all three made their headquarters in the ships of their supporting naval commanders. Thus, Ian Hamilton was with the naval Commander-in-Chief, Admiral de Roebeck in the *Queen Elizabeth*; Birdwood was in the *Queen* with Rear-Admiral Thursby, who was directing the naval part of the Anzac operation; and Hunter-Weston was with Admiral Wemyss in *Euryalus*. They were all three, therefore, obeying one of the principles of a combined operation—that their head-quarters should also be combined. As the Navy was providing the covering fire, that would have seemed sensible. But of course the *Queen Elizabeth* was a fighting ship with her own duties to perform, and she was so large that she couldn't stand in close to shore to give the C-in-C a closer look at what was happening.

It must be remembered that the 'adequate signalling equip-ment' wasn't provided for this hurriedly equipped operation; but even if it had been, Ian Hamilton had, rightly or wrongly, com-mitted almost all his troops to the various landings and feint landings which constituted his plan. He then had to delegate all tactical authority to his two corps commanders. Early in the morning of the invasion Admiral Roger Keyes, seeing through his telescope that the landing on Y beach appeared to have been entirely unopposed (which was quite correct), had urged Ian Hamilton to send for the Naval Division at once and land it at Y beach. This division had been committed to nothing more than a feint in Suvla Bay. The idea of committing his only reserve to a subordinate commander's battle, without his knowledge or consent, was quite abhorrent to Hamilton, who turned it down at once. However, in this case, if Ian Hamilton had agreed and put Roger Keyes in command of the whole operation, with authority to override the orders under which the commander at Y beach was operating—which were to stand still and do nothing—then it might well have been very successful and could have had a decisive effect if—and again it is a big 'if'—it could have been done before the landings at W and V beaches had been so desperately shattered. Anyway, the Y beach landing could not have been worse than it turned out to be. So, with hindsight, Ian Hamilton would have done well to have taken Roger Keyes's advice—particularly as he could see from his conning tower in the *Queen Elizabeth* that the landings at W and V beaches were meeting desperate resistance.

Ian Hamilton and his two subordinate commanders should have been in small ships, completely divorced from the warships engaged in the action—provided, of course, that the military commanders had senior naval liaison officers with them so that the two services could be kept in the closest touch.

There is also the criticism that at W and V beaches, where the really ghastly slaughter took place, more and more men were thrown into the cauldron instead of being held back to exploit success elsewhere. The same criticism was made in many of the battles on the Western Front. But in those types of operation it is very difficult indeed to stop in the middle of a carefully planned battle. In an unsuccessful sector of the attack so many of the leaders are killed or wounded that no information comes back, the troops stagger blindly on, and, as long as some of them get through, the attack may even be considered a success.

The most ghastly error, however, of the whole Gallipoli landing operation was that the underwater wire, which was the chief architect of disaster, was never touched at all by the naval bombardment. Also, owing to the flat trajectory of the naval guns covering the operation, they had to cease fire too soon for fear of hitting their own troops. If there had been a break in the bombardment after the first thirty minutes the Turks would have reoccupied their trenches and some indication would have been given as to where they were. When all is said and done, however, and despite all the mistakes made—by no means all of them by the battle commanders—had it not been for the generalship of Mustapha Kemal at the Anzac landing and the supineness of the Y beach landing force, what was undoubtedly a Turkish victory might well have been a qualified British success.

CHAPTER SIX

Gallipoli: the Australian Attack on Lone Pine

After the first landings in Gallipoli had failed to produce the hoped-for breakthrough, the fighting settled into savage, face-to-face trench warfare, grimly repetitive of the situation on the Western Front. Attack after attack was parried, the sickness rate soared and the conditions in which the troops lived and fought became almost unbelievable.

Between 19 May and the end of August 1915 18 VCs were won in Gallipoli and the Dardanelles. Of these the Royal Navy won 1, British units 7, Australians 9, and New Zealand 1.

On 18 May the Turks launched a major assault intended to drive the Anzacs into the sea. On the night of 19/20 May they had infiltrated into the position held by the 14th Battalion of the Australian Imperial Force. Lance-Corporal Albert Jacka of the 14th had taken part in the historic landing at Anzac and was now in one of the forward trenches. When all the other men in his trench had been killed or wounded seven Turks rushed and occupied the trench. Lance-Corporal Jacka at once gallantly attacked them single-handed and killed the whole party, five by rifle fire and two with the bayonet. Lance-Corporal Jacka's VC was the first awarded in the First World War to a soldier of the Australian and New Zealand Army Corps. Later he served on the Western Front as a lieutenant and won the Military Cross.

Early in August 1915 came the incident at Lone Pine Trenches,

Gallipoli, where seven Australians—2nd Lieutenant William John Symons, Corporal Alexander Stewart Burton, Corporal William Dunstan and Captain Frederick Harold Tubb of the 7th Battalion AIF; Captain Alfred John Shout and Private Leonard Keyzor of the 1st Battalion; and Private John Hamilton of the 3rd Battalion —all won the Victoria Cross. These seven men performed prodigies of valour. Captain Shout lost his right hand and left eye and succumbed to his wounds. Lieutenant Tubb was wounded in the head and arm. Private Keyzor was twice wounded and Corporal Burton was killed.

The attack was launched by the 1st Australian Brigade (1st, 2nd, 3rd and 4th Battalions) on the evening of 6 August. In order to hold the ground gained, the Australians had to throw in units of 2 and 3 Brigades. The 1st Australian Brigade was commanded by Brigadier-General Nevill Maskelyne Smyth, VC, who had won his Cross at Khartoum in the Sudan on 2 September 1898. During the three nights and days of this very desperate close-quarter struggle many deeds of valour were done, both by the Australians and the Turks, who had already proved themselves to be some of the toughest fighters British troops had ever encountered.

This operation—which was part of the second great attempt to take the Gallipoli peninsula—was planned as a feint designed to prevent the Turkish commander from reinforcing his troops defending the heights of Sari Bair, against which the main Anzac attack was to be made. A similar feint was to be launched by the British at Cape Helles, while at Suvla Bay, four miles north of Anzac, 9 Corps (10th and 11th Divisions) would land and try to seize a semicircle of hills five miles inland.

The British High Command realised that the Turks regarded Lone Pine as one of the main points in their defensive system and were confident that they would fight strongly to retain it. That was the object of the exercise. The Turkish trenches at Lone Pine could be clearly seen from the Australian trenches, which were on the same plateau. The highly built up Turkish parapet showed clearly above the sparse, low scrub which separated the two trench systems. The centre of the enemy's defence position was less well advanced than the flanks. Recent air photos of Lone Pine showed that the southern half of the trenches had been roofed over.

The 1st Australian Brigade attack was made on a three-battalion front, the 2nd on the right, or southern, flank; the 3rd in the centre; and the 4th on the left, or northern, flank. The 1st Battalion was in reserve. Each assaulting battalion attacked in three lines. The foremost line started from a secret underground line only 40–60yd from the Turks' front-line trench. In front of parts of their trenches the Turks had constructed a fairly strong wire entanglement. To destroy this and to break down the head-cover over the Turkish trenches a preliminary bombardment was staged, extending over three days. This was nothing like the shattering bombardments known later in France—there were neither the guns nor the ammunition in Gallipoli; but here there were not the same formidable defence system, the masses of machine-guns or the acres of barbed wire which characterised the French battlefields.

Very little damage was done to the Turkish wire entanglement on the first day; but by 3 pm on 6 August, after 383 rounds in all had been fired, most of the wire had been destroyed. During the night of 5/6 August star shells were fired to prevent the enemy from repairing the damage. At 2 pm on the 6th the engineers were withdrawn from the forward tunnels and three mines were exploded in no-man's-land. At 2.30 pm the battalions of the 1st Australian Infantry Brigade moved forward to take up their allotted positions for the assault. At 4 pm the offensive began at Helles, the plumes of earth thrown up by the big naval shells leaping out against the distant skyline. At 4.30 the intensive bombardment at Anzac began.

At this time the three assault battalions of the 1st Australian Brigade at Lone Pine were still moving into their assault positions. Brigadier-General Smyth installed his battle headquarters in a dip immediately behind the forward trenches. The men of the three assaulting battalions wore broad white armlets and white calico squares on their backs for recognition purposes in the dark. They quipped and chaffed one another as they formed up and awaited the 'off' signal. At 5.27 they pulled down the top row of sandbags and then the blowing of a whistle signalled the start of this very desperate and heroic adventure.

At once rifle shots rang out from the Turkish trenches gradually growing into a heavy fusillade. At the same time a tremendous fire came from Australian units on the flanks to keep the enemy's heads down. The leading companies of the two left assaulting battalions were soon into the enemy's forward trench. Only a line of Australian dead on the right showed that part of the 2nd Battalion had been caught in the open. As soon as the forward companies got into the Lone Pine defensive system they found themselves in completely unknown territory. There were the front-line trenches, many of them with head-cover and loopholes which the bombardment had left practically unbroken; and behind them was a system of support trenches, communication trenches and tunnels. In order to avoid the bombardment, nearly half the Turkish garrison had been withdrawn into the tunnels and other shelters. The preliminary bombardment had caused severe losses in the crowded Turkish trenches and the heavy head-cover had increased the effect of the shelling. The Australian attack had come upon the Turks too swiftly to allow them to man their defensive positions, to which they were now returning. Despite the fact that they should have been warned by the actions of the Australians during the week previous to the attack, the Turks never believed that it was anything more than an artillery demonstration. So they were completely surprised when the look-outs in the front line shouted that the Australian infantry were advancing.

The Australian forward companies became so mixed up in the maze of trenches that the boundaries between battalions became blurred. On the left the 4th Battalion met fierce Turkish counter-attacks. It was stark bomb and bayonet work, with no quarter asked or given. The leadership of the Australian company and platoon commanders was magnificent—but costly. Each trench captured was barricaded but was at once subjected to counter-attack. The 3rd Battalion in the centre found the wire entanglements well beaten down but also met with strong Turkish counter-attacks. However, before dark they had established themselves in a series of defensive posts. On the right the 2nd Battalion, having suffered initial casualties, had captured the front Turkish system and pressed forward to the objective which had been given to them. Thus, by 6 pm on the evening of the 6th, the three attacking battalions of the 1st Brigade had established themselves in the Pine, holding a long communication trench on either flank and seven or eight isolated posts in the centre. These posts, spread across the captured position, like the knuckles of an outstretched hand, constituted a formidable defence.

The Turks began to pull themselves together and massed for a counter-attack against the 3rd Battalion in the centre. Major McConaghy, in charge of the 3rd Battalion, called for reinforcements and General Smyth sent him part of his reserve, the 1st Battalion. The remainder of the 1st Battalion was sent up to reinforce the 2nd Battalion on the right. They could not get forward as a stream of wounded men were coming down the communication trenches, so Captain Jacobs took the leading company of the 1st Battalion forward over the open ground. The 12th Battalion was then sent forward to General Smyth to replace the 1st Battalion as his brigade reserve.

The original Turkish garrison of Lone Pine consisted of two battalions of the 47th Regiment, with a third battalion occupying the ridge to the south. At least 500 men held the front-line trenches with another 500 in close support. By 5.30 pm on the 6th, when the Australian attack commenced, about half of the front-line garrison had been killed or wounded and most of the remainder were in the tunnels. As soon as the Australian infantry attack had been launched the 1st Battalion of the 57th Turkish Regiment was immediately moved up to the Pine. There also arrived at the same time the commander of the 13th Turkish Regiment, which had been ordered to retake the position lost at Lone Pine at all costs. The attack of the 1st Australian Brigade had therefore succeeded beyond anticipation in its main object. Essad Pasha, the Turkish Commander, was now so convinced that Lone Pine was the main British offensive that he not only ordered up the 13th Regiment but instructed the whole 9th Turkish Division, stationed between Helles and Anzac, to move in that direction also. The main object of the Turkish commander in the Anzac zone was now to recapture the Lone Pine position.

Meanwhile the battalions of the 1st Australian Infantry Brigade were digging in and strengthening the somewhat scattered positions they had gained. Now the front-line Australian troops began to sustain the first phase of the long and bitter Turkish counter-attack, for which the battle of Lone Pine is chiefly famous. To start with, pressure came against the centre sector. During the morning of the 7th this pressure—confined chiefly to bombing—became intensified. Colonel Macnaghten, CO of the 4th Battalion, was wounded. A good supply of bombs was essential for the Australian resistance, but by now nothing could live in the open and the trenches became blocked with wounded coming down the line and reinforcements going up, and there was a danger that the supply of bombs might be delayed.

By midday on 7 August the Australian front in the northern sector, held by the 4th Battalion, consisted of three blocked sapheads. At each of them bombing continued intermittently until 10 August but they were not again heavily attacked. The main Turkish attack on the 7th and the following days was directed entirely against the centre and southern part of the position. The most dangerous and effective Turkish weapon was the hand grenade. The Australians were eager to reply in kind but they were not only short of bombs but also of trained bomb throwers. By early morning of the 7th the bomb factory near the beach had sent forward all the grenades in stock. The 'Mills' grenade, which became so familiar to the troops in France, was not available in Gallipoli. The bombs in use there by the Australians were crude and rather dangerous missiles to the unskilled thrower, manufactured at a so-called factory on the beach. Jam tins were used as casings and were filled with explosives and pieces of jagged metal, with a fuse to be lit before throwing. The Turkish bombs were cast-iron missiles, about the size and shape of a cricket ball, also with an external fuse of a few seconds' duration.

Only on the extreme right, or southern, sector did the Turks actually get out of their trenches and attack across the open. They were met with a shattering blaze of fire which drove them back, but they returned to the attack, supported by artillery fire. Colonel Scobie of the 2nd was on the spot, encouraging his men, but two of his officers were killed and three wounded, so Colonel Scobie decided that they must withdraw. He remained to see this carried out and was killed by a Turkish grenade. Private Leonard Keyzor of the 1st Battalion was indomitable. He was an expert bomb thrower and was familiar with the Australian and Turkish types. He picked up two live Turkish bombs and threw them back. Although he was wounded on the 7th he was in action again at the same place next day and was wounded again. He refused to go to hospital and continued to throw bombs until the situation was relieved. On several occasions he caught the Turkish bombs in flight and hurled them back. His example was most morale-raising to his fellow Australians and he well deserved his award of the Victoria Cross.

Hectic hand-to-hand fighting continued in the right sector. The Turks were so anxious to regain Lone Pine that the 13th Regiment, which was arriving all day of the 7th, was flung into the battle company by company as it arrived. The Australian 2nd and 1st Battalion trenches were literally floored with dead bodies. Colonel Cass, who had just returned after having been wounded at Helles, took Colonel Scobie's place in command of the 2nd Battalion.

In the centre sector, however, which at dawn on the 8th was still largely held by the survivors of the 3rd Battalion, the strain was telling and one of the forward trenches had to be abandoned. The men of the 1st Brigade were now not only almost completely exhausted but also sick with the stench of dead bodies. Yet they never wavered in their determination to hold on, though many fell asleep where they stood. General Smyth therefore ordered part of the 7th Battalion, which had now been allotted to him, to relieve the 1st and 2nd on the right. The 3rd and 4th Battalions still had to be left holding the centre and left sectors, supported by a mixture of men from the 1st and 12th Battalions.

Meanwhile a great effort had been made to clear the trenches of the dead and, during the remainder of the fighting, this unpleasant but most necessary task was performed by the 5th Connaught Rangers. They were employed continuously in dragging the bodies out and carrying them back for burial.

During the midday hours of the 8th Major McConaghy, now commanding the 3rd Battalion in the centre sector, made a determined effort to dig a new front-line trench to connect up the isolated saphead posts. Despite the officer in charge of the digging being killed, this important work was accomplished. On the afternoon of the 8th the remainder of the 7th Battalion, under command of Colonel Elliott, went into the Pine. The Turks attacked them strongly and continuously from that evening until 2 am on the 9th, but they held their ground.

On 9 August, the fourth and last day of the struggle for the Pine, the Turks made a final desperate attempt to drive the Australians out. Starting at 4 am, under intensive covering fire, they launched a violent attack from the junction of the 3rd and 4th Battalions southwards. Encouraged by their officers, the enemy pressed forward with bomb and bayonet along every trench. The Australians replied with everything they had, the officers using their revolvers. This was the fiercest fighting of all and on this one day six Victoria Crosses were won by the 7th, 1st and 3rd Battalions. Deeds of incredible heroism took place. The entire garrison of Captain Jacobs's trench was caught in enfilade by a Turkish machine-gun and killed to a man. Early in the morning of the 9th the reserve companies of the 12th Battalion were put into the Pine and at midday the 5th Battalion was also put in.

That night the Turkish attack upon Lone Pine ended. The four days' fighting had cost the Australians over 2,000 men, including 80 officers. The commanding officers of the 2nd Battalion, Colonel Scobie, and of the 3rd, Colonel Brown, were both killed, and the CO of the 4th, Colonel Macnaghten, was severely wounded. In the 3rd Battalion every officer was hit—except the Quartermaster—including the Medical Officer and the Chaplain. The enemy's losses were even heavier. The Turkish 16th Division was said to have lost 6,930 men.

Once again the Australians had proved themselves to be

magnificent fighting men. The Battle of Lone Pine Trenches became an epic in Australian military history and will always be remembered with pride in the British Commonwealth.

In all, 38 VCs were won in Gallipoli and the Dardanelles—18 by British units; 9 by Australians; 9 by the Royal Navy; 1 by Canada and 1 by New Zealand; while countless other acts of gallantry and devotion to duty occurred, some perhaps un-honoured and unsung.

CHAPTER SEVEN

Gallipoli: Recollections of Sir Reginald Savory and the Evacuation of the Peninsula

A very vivid recollection of the conditions in Gallipoli is given by Lieut-General Sir Reginald Savory, KCIE, DSO, MC, who, at the time, was a regimental officer in the 14th Sikhs. It demonstrates how, in circumstances such as these, which were similar to those on the Western Front, the leadership of junior commanders is all-important.

Savory writes (in a letter to me):

The 14th Sikhs at first were in the Indian Brigade which was in reserve, but as their bivouacs were close to the gun positions, and the guns were constantly in action, the noise was ear-splitting and it was quite impossible to get much sleep. During the next few days there was very heavy fighting and the Turks were making a determined effort to drive the invaders back into the sea. The Indian Brigade was moved from one place to another, ready to plug holes in the front or counter-attack if required. On 4 May they had to reinforce the French, whose Senegalese troops had been driven back. The 14th Sikhs were amazed that the French troops were still wearing the same blue jackets and red trousers they had worn in the Franco-Prussian war.

G

Meanwhile fresh troops had been arriving, and our brigade, which had been at one time the only reserve at Cape Helles, was sent forward to take over its part of the front. We counted ourselves fortunate in not having been sent straight into the attack, but to have had some days in which to adapt ourselves to local conditions.

On 9 May a brigade of Australians was brought to Helles from Anzac. The Indian Brigade was then holding a line of trenches on the extreme left and these Australians had been ordered to attack through us. This meant jumping over our trenches; no mean feat for men in full fighting order. They came along in great heart, while we covered their advance by fire from our trench. Then they swept up to us, jumped our trenches, and surged on. At once a murderous fire broke out. Up came the second line and over our trench they jumped. One of them was slightly wounded and fell back into our trench. As he did so a packet of 'smutty' postcards cascaded out of one of his pockets. We patched him up; collected his postcards; put them back in his breast pocket, buttoned it up securely and sent him back to the aid-post. As he left he thanked us warmly, not only for our skill in first-aid but for returning his cards. His battle was over. His comrades who had advanced so gallantly had faded away under a murderous fire; and soon the few survivors came trickling back into our trench. Once more we were in the front line. That night we sent out patrols and brought in some of the wounded.

It had been another wasted effort; another frontal assault by new troops, in long uncontrollable lines, against an un-reconnoitred position and with no visible objective.

Our British officers started being hit. Two of them went in one day, both of them company commanders. At last I was in the front line. Our trenches were not very deep, and one had to crawl along them. The Turkish snipers were busy and to show one's head above the top was dangerous. There were parts of the line, however, where unseen Turkish snipers could fire right into our trenches and which seldom became known except by trial and error. The next three weeks were spent in digging. By day we deepened our trenches and made them livable and safe; by night we went forward into no-man's-land, dug little trenches, evacuated them before dawn, and the next night dug communication trenches linking up with them and so gradually sapping towards the Turks, until we were within about fifty yards of them.

On 3 June we received orders for a general assault all along the line next day. That night there was little rest. We were busy cleaning all our arms, issuing extra ammunition, and making steps by which each man could easily clamber out of the trench and go forward over the top. The orders were short and clear. At 11 am on 4 June all guns were to bombard the enemy's front line trenches for twenty minutes. Then for ten minutes they were to stop while the infantry were to cheer and wave their bayonets. The object of this was to persuade the enemy to man their trenches. Then the bombardment was to come down again. At noon we were to advance. It all sounded simple enough. The 14th Sikhs were to attack astride the Gully Ravine.

Our guns started registering at 8 am and even before the bombardment began it must have been clear to the enemy that something was about to happen. Their artillery retaliated. One of their shells fell on our parapet and Fowle, my company commander, and I were nearly buried. We both tried to look nonchalant and to pretend that we had not been very shaken. Our breakfast was ruined. We allotted each man his place, opposite the step he had dug for himself the evening before.

It was now 11.30 and time for the cheering to start; but the noise was so great that we could hardly hear it even in our own trench. A few men had been wounded and had to be replaced. Fowle and I took up our positions. He was with the right half of the company so as to liaise with the battalion on our right; and I was in the centre of the left half. There was a void in the pit of my stomach as I waited for the off. And then—twelve noon—blow the whistle—and we were away. From that moment I lost all control of the fighting. The roar of musketry drowned every other sound, except that of the guns. To try to give an order was useless. The nearest man was only a yard or two away but I couldn't see him. Soon I found myself running on alone, except for my little bugler, a young, handsome boy, just out of his teens, who came paddling along behind me to act as a runner and carry messages. Poor little chap. The sooner I could get across no-man's-land and reach the cover of the enemy trenches the better. And then, before I could realise it, I found myself standing on the parapet of a Turkish trench and looking down at a Turk inside it. He was leaning against the back of his trench. There were other Turks on either side of him. Before he could shoot me I jumped in and skewered him with my bayonet. Poor devil! I can see his grimace to this day.

My next recollection was of lying on my back on the parapet with two Turks using my body as a rest over which to shoot at our second line coming forward. I must have been knocked out. When I fully recovered consciousness the Turks had gone. I looked round and saw my little bugler lying dead, brutally mutilated. I could see no one else. My head was bleeding and I was dazed. I walked back towards our trench. There I was picked up by one of our stretcher-bearers, a great burly Sikh with a fair beard who was one of our battalion wrestlers. He slung me over his shoulder and took me back. The next thing I knew I was in the field-ambulance with a doctor bending over me. I had two small wounds in my forehead—probably, he said, caused by a glancing blow from the tip of a bayonet. After three days in the field-ambulance I walked back to Gully Ravine to find my regiment.

On 8 December 1915, having been in hospital in Alexandria following a bad attack of the dreaded dysentery, and then a period of sick leave, Savory rejoined the 14th Sikhs at Anzac, where he had left them three months earlier. He records:

They were nearly up to strength, having received another company of the Maharajah of Patiala's Infantry. The men had been fitted out with winter clothing and an extra blanket per man, which was just as well as they had been experiencing freezing conditions with blizzards of sleet and snow. Our

trenches were in the low-lying ground and had acted as storm-
drains. All the water from the hills came swishing down into
our trenches. A 'tidal wave', waist high, had rushed through,
washing away all before it. Ammunition, food, bedding, and
all the paraphernalia of a regiment had been swamped. By
the time it had drained away and subsided the men were living
in a sea of stinking, glutinous mud. They had at once set about
cleaning out the trenches and searching for missing articles of
equipment and clothing, and then the wind veered to the north
and with it came the snow. It was as much as flesh and blood
could stand. No human, Indian, British or Turk, could stay
in the trenches in these conditions. They clambered out on to
the top and existed miserably in the open within a hundred
yards or so of each other. Both sides were too concerned with
keeping warm and salvaging such things as they needed, to
bother about firing at one another. Then came the frost. We
in the 14th Sikhs were fortunate in having some new officers
who had come recently from France and knew all about 'trench-
feet' and their treatment, and surprisingly we suffered only
eighteen cases of frost-bite. Our telephone orderly, however,
whose duty compelled him to stay at his post, was found one
morning frozen to death; and many others succumbed to
exposure. Fortunately there was no shortage of rum and the
Sikhs and our friends, the Gurkhas, took full advantage of the
generous issues which were made from the large stocks which
had accumulated.

In October 1915 General Sir Charles Monro, who was then
commanding the 3rd Army in France, was ordered to take over
the command of the Gallipoli operations from General Sir Ian
Hamilton. (General Sir George Barrow gives a very clear picture
of these happenings in his biography of General Monro.) From
August 1914, when Monro went to France as a divisional
commander, his reputation had been steadily growing and his
appointment received unqualified approval. Although he appeared
in the Gallipoli drama only in the last scene, he certainly played
a vital part. Gallipoli had all along been the subject of consider-

able political, military and public controversy. Having handed over command of the 3rd Army to Allenby, Monro arrived in London on 20 October and spent most of the next two days in interviews with Lord Kitchener, the Secretary of State for War, and the General Staff.

After months of heroic effort we were no nearer Constantinople than we had been at the start, and the thoughts of the War Cabinet had begun to turn towards the possible necessity for evacuation. Sir Ian Hamilton, when asked for his opinion, said that such a step was 'unthinkable' and that, in any case, we could not get out of Gallipoli without the loss of half the total force, with all the guns, stores and plant.

The War Cabinet, however, decided to recall Ian Hamilton and replace him by a general who, coming with a fresh and un-biased mind, would be better able to advise on the question of evacuation. General Monro was selected for that purpose. Kitchener instructed him to report fully and frankly and as early as possible on the military situation on the Gallipoli peninsula and in the Near East generally, and to give his opinion, on purely military grounds, as to whether it would be better to evacuate Gallipoli or to make another attempt to carry it.

General Monro arrived at Mudros on 27 October and spent three strenuous days going round the positions and making a close inspection of the general situation. On 31 October he wired his report to Kitchener. He reviewed the situation at considerable length and came to the conclusion that, as we still held only the fringe of the shore, with the Turks in formidable entrenchments above us, holding all the dominant points and having complete observation over all our positions, giving us no possibility of surprise attacks, and with the Turkish positions being strengthened daily, it was advisable, 'on purely military grounds', to evacuate the peninsula, 'in consequence of the grave daily wastage of officers and men'.

There was one other factor of importance which served to strengthen Monro's decision. Early in October German, Austrian and Bulgarian armies had swept over Serbia and opened the way for the transport of heavy artillery and munitions of war to strengthen the Turkish defence. Henceforth every day's delay would favour the enemy rather than us, and with the advent of guns of heavy calibre in the Turkish lines our situation on the beaches would become increasingly untenable.

However, after General Monro had been asked to give his opinion on purely military grounds, his report was at once thrown into the political arena, and the first person who began to weaken under the political broadside of Mr Churchill and others was Kitchener himself. He cabled to Monro on 1 November to ask whether the corps commanders agreed with his opinion. This was a quite extraordinary procedure. Having selected a high-ranking commander of outstanding repute to give his own opinion and then to ask for the opinions of his subordinates was an obvious sign of no confidence. And the natural result, as far as General Monro was concerned, was to shake his confidence in Lord Kitchener. The latter had gone even further. On 3 November he cabled to one of Monro's corps commanders, General Bird-wood: 'I absolutely refuse to sign orders for evacuation, which I think would be the gravest disaster and would condemn a large percentage of our troops to death and imprisonment.'

If Kitchener felt so violently against evacuation, why had he sent General Monro to report 'fully and frankly' on the situation? However, Monro could only obey the orders of his superiors and he called on his three corps commanders 'to give their opinions without paying any heed to his'.

Generals Davies and Byng agreed with him and Birdwood didn't. In view of the latter's cable from Kitchener of 3 November he could hardly have done anything else. The very wobbly War Committee of the Cabinet, buffeted by the waves of contradictory opinions, asked Lord Kitchener to go out to Gallipoli himself and give his own opinion. Kitchener, casting aside all the ethics of military behaviour, cabled to Birdwood that Monro would be removed from the Gallipoli command, that Birdwood would succeed, and that he was on his way to visit him. At the same time Kitchener cabled to Monro: 'You have been appointed to the command of Salonika force. General Birdwood will take over from you the command of the Mediterranean Force.' The unfortunate General Monro, in the space of a few weeks, had been removed from command of an army in France, entrusted with a special mission which he had carried out with fearless judgement, and had received a very unjustified slap in the face. To add to his troubles, he had had one of his ankles smashed in disembarking from a naval launch and never entirely regained the use of that leg.

Lord Kitchener inspected the positions at Helles, Anzac and Suvla on 12, 13 and 14 November, and on 15 November sent a telegram to the Prime Minister which constituted a complete vindication of Monro's judgement. It finished up with the words: 'In present circumstances the raison d'être of our forces on the Gallipoli Peninsula is no longer as important as it has been hitherto. Careful and secret preparations for the evacuation of the Peninsula are being made.'

The final evacuation of the peninsula in January 1916 was an unbelievable success, wonderfully planned and conducted by Birdwood, de Roebeck and Keyes, the three men who had been there from the beginning. The last troops departed silently and not a man was left behind.

So General Monro was completely vindicated, and he was given command of the 1st Army in France. But some of the mud stuck, and that, together with his immobility occasioned by his accident in Gallipoli, resulted in the end of his career as a battle commander. In 1916 he went as Commander-in-Chief to India. After the war he had a period of six years as Governor of Gibraltar.

Out of the 410,000 British troops who had been engaged in the Gallipoli campaign there had been 205,000 casualties. The Turks admitted to 251,000 casualties from their 500,000 men engaged.

Ian Hamilton had been relieved of the Gallipoli command in October 1915. He did not hold another active military appointment. He died in October 1947 at the age of ninety-four.

Birdwood went on to command an army in France and after the war he became Commander-in-Chief in India, where he was as much loved by the Indian troops as he had been by the Anzacs.

CHAPTER EIGHT

The Battles of Loos and of the Somme

The ill-fated battle of Loos, which began on the morning of 25 September 1915, illustrates most vividly how the flouting of established principles of war on the part of the higher command can bring disaster in its train and unnecessary slaughter to the unfortunate troops involved.

Although Sir John French was much criticised for this debâcle it is only fair to say that he had been opposed to the attack from the start, but was forced, on the instructions of the British Government, to make the attack at the request of Marshal Joffre in conformity with the latter's general offensive. So, in August, Haig's 1st Army was ordered to relieve the French troops on its right, the British 4 Corps taking over the lines opposite Loos.

The attack was to be made by Rawlinson's 4 Corps. Rawlinson was also strongly opposed to this attack because he did not consider that we should go on hammering at the German trenches until our resources—particularly in material—had greatly increased. He also remarked:

My new front at Loos is as flat as the palm of my hand. Hardly any cover anywhere. Easy enough to hold defensively but very difficult to attack. Douglas Haig tells me that we are to attack 'au fond', that the French are doing likewise and making a supreme effort. It will cost us dearly and we shall not get very far. *(The Life of Lord Rawlinson,* p 137)

Rawlinson was, as usual, more acutely aware of the situation and the factors involved than any of the other British generals. He would have favoured his 'bite and hold' policy here, but he had to subordinate his personal views and carry out loyally the plan decided upon by his superiors. The result of the initial attack raised high hopes, but Sir John French's decision to keep the two follow-up divisions well back was fatal. The only hope of an attack 'au fond' being successful was for the reserve divisions to be ready to go through and carry on the momentum before the inevitable German counter-attack took place. But French did not place the 21st and 24th Divisions at Haig's disposal until the morning of the 26th, twenty-four hours after the attack of the forward divisions had started.

Rawlinson had detailed the first two divisions of the new Kitchener's Army to be committed to battle—the 15th Highland and the 47th. Rawlinson had written to Kitchener on 6 August:

> You will be interested to hear something about the Highland Division, commanded by McCracken [later General Sir F. W. McCracken], which has lately joined my Corps and has now taken over a section of the front line. The men are, I fancy, the best that have come out of the Highlands and I never saw finer battalions than the 6th and 7th Camerons and the 8th Seaforths. What has struck me most is the stamp of company officers, which is far better than I had expected; and the pioneer battalion, in the shape of the 9th Gordons, has proved excellent both in the way of trench construction and as a fighting unit.

To add to the anxieties which surrounded this battle of Loos it had been decided that, for the first time, the British were to use gas and smoke screens with their preliminary artillery bombardment. The anxieties inseparable from the use of gas discharged from cylinders were, first, whether the enemy would discover that the cylinders had been taken up into the trenches; and second, and all-important, whether the wind would be blowing in the right direction at the time of the attack. The weather had been changeable, and at 1 am on the night of 24/25 August Sir Douglas

Haig had to take the vital decision as to whether the attack should proceed or be postponed. His weather expert, who was in touch with the meteorological forecasts in both France and England, came to the conclusion that there was more chance of a south-west wind on the morning of the 25th than there would be on the 26th, and as Joffre was very anxious that the British attack should go in on the morning of the 25th, it was wisely decided that it should take place as arranged.

When the Germans had launched their first chlorine gas attack at Ypres in April 1915 the wind had been strongly in their favour. The main reason, however, why they had discontinued using heavier-than-air gas from cylinders was because the prevailing wind was generally against them. When the gas was released at 4.50 am on the 25th at Loos, with a cloudy sky and slight drizzle it gradually drifted towards the German trenches in a huge white and yellow cloud, rising to a height of 300ft. As it reached the German trenches it mingled with volumes of white smoke created by the phospher bombs fired by the British trench mortars. At one point only, on the right of the 1st Division, the gas drifted back and about 200 men and five officers of the 60th Rifles were overcome by the fumes. The assault of 2 Brigade at this point failed. The 15th Division, who were in the centre, well supported by the artillery, rushed straight on through the village of Loos, over Hill 70 and on to Cité St-Auguste. The 47th Division on the right, charging forward with equal dash, gained all their objectives and formed a flank covering the right of the 15th Division. The 1st Division did not gain their objectives until 4 pm, and then only after hard fighting in which they finally captured 700 prisoners.

There can be no doubt that the enemy were surprised by the vigour of the first rush of these three divisions, and had they been immediately supported by the 21st and 24th Divisions, who were ready at Noeux-les-Mines for the purpose, they might have gained possession of the enemy's second system of defences. As it was, they arrived too late to take any part in the fighting on the 25th, by which time the 1st and 15th Divisions, which had actually entered the enemy's third line of defences, had been forced to withdraw.

It was not until 11 am on the 26th that the 21st and 24th Divisions were launched into the attack. But the ever-aggressive and efficient Germans had by that time been able to organise a devastating fire plan with artillery and machine-guns against both flanks of the attack. These two divisions, caught on the open plain with no adequate artillery support, were subjected to such a hail of fire that they turned and retired in one huge mass, back through our original trench line and on to the neighbourhood of Vermelles and Philosophe before they could be rallied. The attack had ended in disastrous failure. General Rawlinson considered that if these two new divisions could have been brought into the battle between 10 and 11 am on the morning of the 25th they might well have broken right through.

Although Sir John French had been against an attack at Loos, the disaster which ensued was entirely due to the fact that he had refused to put the two reserve divisions, right from the start, at the disposal of Rawlinson, who alone could estimate when the psychological moment had arrived for their employment. And had Rawlinson been allowed to 'bite and hold', the battle of Loos could have been, on a limited scale, a brilliant success. With well-planned gas, smoke and artillery support the first attack was successful: with no gas and no planned artillery support, and after twenty-four hours' delay, the second attack hadn't a chance.

Coming up into the Loos battle area after the attack, a machine-gunner of the 6th Battalion the Queen's Royal West Surrey Regiment, writes as follows:

Wrecked war gear lay about on both sides as we edged forward, including field guns, limbers and dead horses by the score. Blown up by internal gases, their carcasses were enormous, and when punctured by shrapnel or bullets the foulest stench poisoned the air. At last we reached the top of a slope and there, stretching for several hundred yards on the right of the road, lay masses of British dead, struck down by machine guns and rifle fire. Shells from enemy field batteries had been pitching into the bodies flinging some about into dreadful postures. Being mostly of Highland regiments there was a fantastic display of colour from their kilts, glengarries and bonnets, and also from the bloody wounds on their bare limbs. The warm weather had darkened their faces, and, shrouded as they were with the sickly odour of death, it was repulsive to be near them.

Hundreds of rifles lay about, some stuck in the ground on the bayonet, as though impaled at the very moment of the soldier's death as he fell forward. In the distance, three kilometres south, and in the midst of concentrated shell bursts, I could just discern the huge twin-tower steel structure known to the troops as 'Tower Bridge'. It stood at a pithead near the village of Loos and when captured by the British threatened the enemy as an observation post. It received a heavy battering for a few days and its end was only a matter of time.

One morning, when looking towards Loos, when a fierce rumpus was going on, I noticed that the thing had gone.

(George Coppard, *With a Machine Gun to Cambrai*)

On 19 December 1915 Douglas Haig became Commander-in-Chief in France in place of Sir John French, and on 23 December General Robertson became Chief of the Imperial General Staff in London. Kitchener remained as Secretary of State for War but with considerably reduced powers, having handed over the strategical side to the CIGS. Robertson had agreed to accept the appointment only if the terms of a memorandum, which he himself had composed, were agreed. The essence of it was as follows. A supreme directing authority or War Council—not to be confused with the Cabinet Advisory Committee—would be set up to formulate policy, choose the men to execute that policy, and supervise the conduct of the war. The War Council was to receive all advice on matters concerning military operations through one authoritative channel only—the CIGS. The latter would issue and sign all operation orders, and all communications from general officers commanding in the field were to be addressed to him. The Secretary of State for War would confine himself to the raising, maintenance and equipment of troops.

This brought to an end the complete dominance of Lord Kitchener who, in a civil appointment, had worn uniform and directed the generals in the field as well as the War Office at home. He had done a wonderful job and borne an immense burden in the early days of the war and his prestige was terrific. He alone had foreseen that the war would be a long one and had made provision accordingly. But Kitchener was not a strategist and, in any case, the war had got too big for one man to control.

Robertson now assumed a vital position in the conduct of the war. He and Haig were both 'Westerners'—convinced that the war could be won only on the Western Front and that all possible military effort should be directed there. And he and Haig were close friends and saw eye to eye on almost everything.

Haig took up a greater burden and bigger responsibility than ever faced a British commander, before or since: and he not only carried it continuously to the end of the war but was at his very best in the vital closing stages when many another man might have been completely worn out. Moreover, he retained throughout the confidence of the British Army, most of the British generals, the Unionist party in the House of Commons and the British people. That is not to say that some of his decisions and his battles were not extremely controversial, nor that he always had the backing of his political masters. Both Lloyd George and Winston Churchill were at times very critical of him indeed—and Lloyd George would have gladly seen him replaced, and did eventually succeed in curtailing his powers quite considerably. But Haig had many friends in high places, was tremendously robust and not easily defeated—either by the Germans or by his own critics. He was a skilful publicist. He won over influential Members of Parliament who visited his headquarters in France, and took frequent leaves home where he kept in touch with the politicians. He was always in close touch with Asquith and other leaders of the Liberal party. He had the warm support of the king, who interested himself in military matters much more influentially than have any of his successors. And, not least in importance, Haig took trouble with the Press and knew how to handle it. He also took particular trouble with the leading French politicians, who generally supported him.

Haig's great inward strength lay in the fact that he was completely dedicated to beating the Germans. He realised that they were a rough and tough enemy. He was resolved to be rougher and tougher—and to continue attacking them at every opportunity with relentless vigour. The cost of his policy in casualties and munitions of war was colossal. But, provided that the Germans suffered as much or more, he was content. And in the end his policy paid off and it was the Germans who started to wilt. It can never be proved whether the Germans would have wilted sooner if the British offensives had not been so costly in men, or if some had not been undertaken at all. However, Haig's great anxiety was that the French, who had suffered such ghastly casualties in the first weeks of the war, would not stick it out. At times the morale of the French troops sank very low indeed. Many of Haig's offensives were embarked upon with the primary object of taking pressure off them.

The people who visited Haig's headquarters were legion; British and French prime ministers and generals were constant visitors; also the king—and the queen—and the French president. What a contrast to Montgomery's austere caravan in the North African campaign in the Second World War! Through it all, Haig went on his own well-ordered way, realising that he would have to pace himself strictly to stay the course: he was convinced that he had a mission to achieve victory and that only he could do it. Haig was a deeply religious man and his faith was a great comfort to him. At this time he had a tendency to asthma and bronchitis and was subject to bouts of malaria. He enjoyed good food and good wine but in strict moderation. He kept regular hours, never missed his full night's sleep and went horse riding at every opportunity. He was a sensitive man and couldn't bear to visit the wounded in hospital or in dressing stations: it made him physically sick. He was not a good speaker and avoided giving addresses, although he wrote clearly and well. He had little personal magnetism, but much enthusiasm, and he exuded confidence. Most people thought he was rather remote, but his staff were devoted to him.

Lieutenant-General Sir Philip Neame, VC, KBE, CB, DSO, considered that Smith-Dorrien and Rawlinson were two of the finest First World War generals. Neame also had a very high opinion of General Plumer, who was his Army Commander for the last six months of the war, when Neame was GSO of the 10th Division. Neame says:

> Plumer had a wonderful gift of getting in touch with his troops, despite the vast size of modern armies and the immense area they cover. He was affectionately known to them as 'Plum' or 'Old Plum' and everyone who knew him liked him. They also liked being in Second Army and felt that they would have a good show in any battle directed by him. When my division was on its way to take over the Mont Rouge–Mont Noir sector, near Mont Kemmel, which had just been lost by its French garrison, 'Plum' came and inspected all our brigades in turn, walking along the ranks and talking here and there to the soldiers.   (*Playing with Strife*)

Neame is bitterly critical of certain war correspondents who denigrated Plumer as an old fuddy duddy—simply because he had grey hair and a red face and didn't go out of his way to ingratiate himself with them. Certainly there was no general of the First World War for whom the troops had more affection and confidence than Plumer.

Neame also had a high opinion of Haig. Soon after Neuve Chapelle, Neame, then a junior Sapper officer, who had won a wonderful VC a few months earlier, was given the job of building one of the first strong redoubts for all-round defence close behind our front line. General Rawlinson, the corps commander, came up to see it, as did the army commander, Douglas Haig. Neame says:

> We juniors of course felt this a great honour and also, not knowing Haig and his habits, thought it very near the front line for an Army Commander. Soon after he reached the redoubt the Germans started shelling. Haig's staff at once became very agitated and one of them asked me to hurry round so that the General could get away. But Haig went on,

perhaps a little slower than before, quite unmoved and taking an intimate interest in every detail of the work. He had no intention of being hurried by German shells and gave us good advice and helpful criticism. He had the reputation of being shy and reserved, but he was very pleasant, even charming, when out with his troops, and knew exactly how to deal with all ranks and impress his great personality on those under his command. I could imagine no finer commander for British troops when they were up against it. He may not have been a military genius such as Marlborough or Napoleon but he was a great strategist and a most determined fighter and commander.

Above all else Haig was devoted to his wife. He took regular leave home which he spent in her flat in London, though of course he had a number of official engagements in London as well. But it is not my intention to make out that he was a saintly character. He was disloyal in thought and word, though not in deed, to his chief, Sir John French, in the early part of the war, and intrigued constantly to get him removed and himself appointed in his place. He was antagonistic to Kitchener and later to his prime minister, Lloyd George, but his excuse was always that he was acting for the good of the cause—the defeat of the Germans—and he may well have been right.

One most remarkable thing about Haig was his diary, which he wrote up almost every day at considerable length. He had been an inveterate diarist all his life, but only during the war did he write a diary on this scale. He is the only general in the field in our history to have done so. (Alanbrook, when Chief of Staff, also kept a diary in the Second World War, but it was not nearly so voluminous as Haig's.) Even when he was at his busiest he seldom let more than a day or two go past without putting down his doings and his thoughts on paper. He used an ordinary field service notebook and he made a carbon copy of everything he wrote. Every four or five days he would tear out the carbon copies and send them, with a personal letter, by King's Messenger to his wife in England. The sheer assiduity of this for a man in his position is quite fantastic. The complete diary ran to at least three-

H

quarters of a million words. The most important part of it was the political side; his relations with the Crown, the Cabinet, the War Office, the Press and the Allies. After the war ended Haig had his diary typed out and bound in thirty-eight substantial volumes in which he also incorporated a large number of letters, which he had sent or received, together with telegrams, despatches, appreciations and memoranda. These volumes were deposited in the British Museum.

In 1952 Robert Blake compressed about one-fifth of the diaries into a book called *The Private Papers of Douglas Haig*. The written word of what a commander thought about his campaign *at the time* is not only very revealing but quite invaluable from a historical point of view. Many commanders have written books about their campaigns, or other people have written them, years after the events, when time has not only mellowed their thoughts and opinions but has allowed alterations to be made, obvious errors to be corrected, and perhaps harsh criticisms to be toned down.

Haig had a great ally in King George V who visited him in France on many occasions, and to whom he unburdened himself freely, both in conversation and in writing.

Haig was faintly amused at the king's pledge not to touch alcohol until the end of the war. He remarked that perhaps the king had made it before he knew how long the war would last. 'Did you hear', Haig wrote to his wife, 'how poor Lord Rosebery got such a hiccough after drinking one glass of ginger beer at the Royal table at Windsor that he could not talk to the Queen?' But, on 11 August 1914, when the king lunched at GHQ and had asked that only soft drinks should be served, there was almost a breakdown in the Entente Cordiale. Haig wrote in his diary: 'Many of us will long remember General Joffre's look of abhorrence when my butler asked him if he would like lemonade or ginger beer.' Fortunately Mr Prime Minister Asquith was not present on this occasion.

Asquith stood very high in Haig's regard, and this was reciprocated. Haig wrote in his diary on 11 September 1916:

Mr Asquith has such a clear and balanced mind. Even in his

cups he is never fuddled. You [Lady Haig] would have been amused at the PM last night. He seemed to like our old brandy. He had a couple of big glasses before I left the table at 9.30 and several more afterwards. By that time his legs were unsteady but his head was quite clear and he was able to read a map and discuss the situation with me.

In the early days of the war Asquith paid a visit to the battle-front in France and wanted to inspect some of the troops— including a detachment from my own battalion. One of my fellow subalterns complained bitterly that a whole day of our precious few days in rest billets should be taken up by a long march to some French village where we were to be inspected by the prime minister. It was a cold and rainy day but I was young, patriotic and burning with British ardour and I took such complaints as insulting. But as the time of the inspection was postponed from 2 pm to 2.30 pm, from 2.30 to 3, and then from 3 to 3.30, my enthusiasm began to wane. And when my fellow subaltern suggested that the prime minister had lunched too well, I did not reply to him as crushingly as I might have done earlier in the day. And then, at long last, he was there. A faint cheer rose from the bored and weary troops. But the prime minister did not get out of the car; he did not even stop. And it was quite obvious to all of us that Mr Asquith had indeed lunched too well. It took me a long time to regain my faith in political leaders!

When, at the end of 1916, Asquith fell from power, Haig wrote: 'I am personally very sorry for poor old Squiff. He has had a hard time and even when "exhilarated" seems to have had much more capacity and brain power than any of the others.'

Haig was not an admirer of Winston Churchill who was by no means such a confirmed Westerner as he was himself. But they made friends later in the war.

Haig's decision to launch the mammoth offensive on the Somme, which started on the morning of 1 July 1916, has always been the subject of great controversy. The assault was entrusted to Sir Henry Rawlinson's 4th Army, but the general conduct of the battle was decided by Haig. As far back as 5 March Haig had been urged by Joffre to stage a major offensive north of the Somme to ease the pressure on the French at Verdun. French forces were to co-operate with the British.

In April Haig crossed to England to acquaint the Government with the proposed major combined offensive and obtain its authority to proceed. Agreement was obtained and the planning between Haig and Joffre went ahead. Certain differences between them had first to be resolved. When Haig mentioned 15 August as his proposed date for the offensive to start, Joffre blew up and shouted: 'The French Army will have ceased to exist if we do nothing until then.' (*Soldier True*, p 172.) Joffre wanted a series of 'wearing-down' engagements before the main attack in order to draw in and consume the enemy reserves. He also made it clear that he wanted the British to do the main job, since the French had already suffered enormous losses and were running short of men. Haig disagreed: he preferred an all-out punch to burst the enemy lines, followed by exploitation by the cavalry. For that reason he wanted plenty of time for preparation. Unfortunately, when the punch was finally delivered on 1 July it failed to burst through the German lines and the Somme became a desperate, long-drawn-out battle of attrition, with the most terrible casualties.

Although Haig had been ordered by his own government to conform as far as possible with Joffre in the planning of the Somme battle—and that included the date on which it was to commence— he could well have made a proviso with Joffre regarding the latter. The reason why Haig wanted the starting date postponed from 1 July to 15 August was to give more time for the preparation, particularly of the artillery programme, on which thousands of his soldiers' lives depended. Joffre had a far higher proportion of guns to the extent of frontage and the number of men engaged in the French Army attack than Haig. Haig might well have said that, in view of the crisis which faced the French Army, he would agree to Joffre's starting date provided it was understood that he would not commit British troops to attack strong German positions protected by unbroken wire. In sectors, therefore, where it was plain that this situation existed on 1 July, he would reserve the right, in those sectors, to postpone the attack (but not the artillery bombardment) for a day or more until the defence had been properly dealt with. It could not be of any advantage to the French attack for the British divisions on their flank to produce no more than heaps of corpses, which is what happened.

For Robertson, as for Haig, the Somme represented the first great test of Western strategy. It dominated the thoughts and actions of them both. They both had a tremendous part to play; they were both big men with the same basic ideas and beliefs, but with utterly different backgrounds. Haig was the aristocrat, inwardly secure in his faith in himself, his religion, and above all in his sense of mission to win the war for Britain. He never sought to justify his actions to anyone—except to himself. Robertson was a much more down-to-earth character, with no privilege of birth, money or class, but with tremendous gifts of brain and courage. He judged everyone by what they were and what they did, not just by what they said. He feared nothing and no man.

Books have been written about the Somme and more will be written in days to come. Briefly, Haig's plan was to make an all-out assault on an eighteen-mile front, between Gommecourt in the north and Maricourt in the south, with eighteen divisions belonging to Allenby's 3rd Army and Rawlinson's 4th. The majority of the divisions were New Army volunteers and Territorials, grouped under Rawlinson. On the British right, five French divisions were to attack along the river Somme.

The preliminary bombardment lasted from 24 June till 1 July, when, on a warm and sunny morning, the British troops advanced from their trenches. On this ghastly first day of the Somme the British lost 60,000 men, of whom one-third were killed, and the only success was some small penetration in the southern sector. The French did better, owing chiefly to the fact that they had a much greater artillery concentration for a much smaller front.

And what were the reasons for this British disaster—for disaster it was, despite what Haig and Rawlinson said about it? Instead of the leading waves of attackers being lightly armed men advancing quickly across no-man's-land at the greatest possible speed, they were all heavily loaded, carrying 60lb or more, advancing at a steady pace against defences which were supposed to have been flattened by the big artillery bombardment. However, the slowness of the advance, together with the inadequacy of the bombardment, enabled the German machine-gun crews to emerge from their dugouts and take a terrible toll of the advancing British infantry. The only good thing about the first day of the Somme was the incredible bravery of the young New Army volunteers.

Without doubt, however, there was only one outstanding reason for the disastrous first day of the Somme. The German trench system on this part of the front was exceptionally strong, with well-built dugouts and fronted by masses of wire. There were not enough guns per mile of the British attack frontage, nor was there enough time, to flatten the defence system before the infantry attack was launched. This was proved by the fact that the French Army attack on a much smaller frontage against similar defences, but with a far greater concentration of guns, had much more success.

Private George Coppard, at that time in the 37th Machine Gun Company, recollects the Somme in these words:

On the afternoon of 1st July 1916, a date that will never be forgotten, we passed through Albert on our way to the front and we knew that the great assault had started that morning. There was a terrific congestion of troops and vehicles at Crucifix Corner. The road forked there and in the angle, commanding the approach, stood a huge crucifix. The sorrowful face of Christ gazed down at the turmoil below. Many men who had passed by on their way to the front were now dead; and many more were to follow them. The thunder of the guns and the scream of shells passing close above us was nerve-wracking. It must have been torture for the horses and mules.

At last, just as it was getting dark, we reached the trench from which the attack had started at 7.30 a.m. The next morning we surveyed the dreadful scene in front of our trench. The German line followed points of eminence, always giving a commanding view of No-man's-land. Immediately in front, and spreading left and right until hidden from view, was clear evidence that the attack had been brutally repulsed. Hundreds of dead were strung out like wreckage washed up to a high-water mark. Quite as many had died on the enemy wire as on the ground, like fish caught in a net. They hung there in grotesque postures. Some looked as though they were praying; they died on their knees and the wire had prevented their fall. From the way the dead were equally spread out, whether on the wire or lying in front of it, it was clear that there were no gaps in the wire at the time the infantry attack took place. Concentrated machine gun fire from sufficient guns to command every inch of the wire, had done its terrible work. The German wire was so dense that daylight could barely be seen through it. The German faith in massed wire had paid off. How did our planners imagine that Tommies, having survived all other hazards—and there were plenty in crossing No-man's-land— would get through the German wire? A vast amount of artillery fire was directed against the enemy wire before 1st July but it was largely wasted effort.

In my opinion the German troops were in no way superior to the British. What was superior was the enemy trench system, built in thorough German fashion and defended by large numbers of machine guns. What I saw on the morning of 2nd July made it clear that our chaps could only reach the wire— and then die. Someone had blundered about the wire. Any element of surprise had been ruined by the long bombardment of the enemy trenches, commencing as far back as 2nd June. Jerry thus had ample time to repair and strengthen his defences, and lay doggo in deep dugouts waiting for us.

(*With a Machine Gun to Cambrai*)

Private Coppard was an extremely intelligent man and he has put his finger on the main cause of bitterness against the higher command and the staff. It was not enough to lay on a large number of guns. The assaulting troops should not have been committed to the assault until it had become as certain as possible that the wire had been cut and the forward trench system destroyed; otherwise it was just murder. This bitterness is reflected in a certain change of attitude from the early days, when the war was still a great crusade and men went to their death proudly; an attitude described earlier and epitomised in some of the poetry of Rupert Brooke (who died in 1915 at Gallipoli). Later poets wrote in a different strain. Siegfried Sassoon wrote:

> Good morning, good morning the General said
> When we met him last week on our way to the line.
> Now the soldiers he smiled at are most of them dead
> And we're cursing his staff for incompetent swine.

And:

> If I were fierce and bald and short of breath
> I'd live with scarlet majors at the base
> And speed glum heroes up the line to death.

But the comradeship remained in spite of, or perhaps more strongly because of, the disillusionment. Wilfred Owen wrote:

> By wire and wood and stake we're bound,
> By Fricourt and by Festubert.
> By whipping rain, by the sun's glare,
> By all the misery and loud sound.
> By a Spring day,
> By Picard clay.
> Show me the two so closely bound
> As we, by the wet bond of blood,
> By friendship, blossoming from mud,
> By death: we faced him, and we found
> Beauty in Death,
> In dead men breath.

As so often happened, however, in the First World War, there were many extenuating circumstances on the generals' end for what was generally known as 'the bloodbath of the Somme'. This particular area was considered by the British High Command to be

quite unsuitable for a major offensive as it was well known that the
Germans had constructed an immensely strong system of defence
there. But Joffre was at this time the predominant partner; the
boundary between the French and British armies lay along the
Somme and it was there that Joffre insisted—and Kitchener and
the British War Cabinet supported him—that the British should
be involved in a large-scale offensive for the first time.

So much for the place of the attack. Now as regards timing. For
the British Somme offensive vast dumps had to be accumulated,
camps established, railway lines laid and the troops very carefully
trained. Haig said he would not be ready until 15 August. Joffre
said it was essential for the morale of the French Army that the
attack should be launched much sooner.

So the British were compromised, as to both the place and the
timing of this attack. They were expected to achieve the hardest of
all victories, namely the defeat of an enemy in a defensive position
of exceptional strength, without any real prospect of strategic gain.

Robertson's biographer, Victor Bonham-Carter writes:

> What happened on 1st July is generally regarded as the greatest
> single tragedy of the war. The British failed initially for a variety
> of reasons. The artillery fire, though heavy in comparison with
> the past, was not heavy enough; nor was it otherwise effective.
> There were too few batteries for such a long and deeply extended
> front, too many gun and ammunition failures, no smoke shells
> and hardly any gas. As a result vast damage was done to the
> enemy, especially to his communications, but the first line
> trenches survived while the second line was hardly touched.
> (*Soldier True*)

It is difficult to give an objective—as opposed to an emotional—
answer to the question: 'Was the Somme worth-while?' Judging
by the small extent of ground gained with such appalling casualties,
the answer would be definitely 'No'. A whole generation of British
youth was wiped out or maimed for life and since the men were for
the most part volunteers they included the flower of the nation.
But judged by the long term—the relief it afforded to Verdun and

the boost it gave to the shaky morale of the French Army, and by what the German Chief of Staff, Ludendorff, said, that 'by the end of 1916 the German Army was fought to a standstill and was utterly worn out'—the answer might be different. In the final reckoning it could be argued that had it not been for the Somme the German Army might never have lost the war. Conversely it might well be argued that had it not been for the Somme the Allied armies might have won it sooner.

All hopes of a quick breakthrough had gone, but the offensive continued at a slower tempo. All through July and August fresh attacks were mounted in one sector or another. In September prospects improved and, on the 15th, Haig launched a major attack, employing tanks for the first time. Many of the tanks were knocked out or failed mechanically, but their moral effect was terrific. But considerable criticism was levelled at whoever was responsible for using them so prematurely and in such small numbers, thus squandering all the element of surprise.

Mr Churchill, in his *World Crisis 1916–1918*, says of the employment of tanks in the battle of the Somme: 'To achieve this miniature success and to carry the education of the professional mind one stage further forward, a secret of war which, well used, would have procured a world-shaking victory in 1917, had been recklessly revealed to the enemy.'

Rawlinson was not of this opinion (*The Life of Lord Rawlinson of Trent*, p 226). He would in fact never have dared to attempt with the tanks of 1916 what he attempted with the tanks of 1918; and it was the experience gained in 1916 which enabled the tanks of 1918 to be produced. Nor is Mr Churchill's opinion shared by any of the tank experts. Colonel Fuller, the great tank expert,* in his *Tanks in the Great War* (p 59), after reciting the lessons learnt on the Somme, has this to say:

These are the main lessons learnt from the tank operations which took place during the battles of the Somme and the Aisne, and

* Colonel Fuller was my senior teacher when I was a student at the Staff College Camberley in 1923–4. He was acknowledged to be, as well as the leading tank expert, one of the finest brains in the Army.

the mere fact of having learnt them justified the employment of tanks during these operations. Further it must be remembered that, whatever tests are carried out under peace conditions, the only true test of efficiency is war, consequently the final test a machine or weapon should get is its first battle. Until this test has been undergone no guarantee can be given of its real worth and no certain deductions can be made as to its future improvement.

During the second half of 1916 some famous Victoria Crosses were won. Captain (Temporary Lieut-Colonel) Adrian Carton de Wiart, DSO, of the 4th Dragoon Guards, attached 8th Battalion Gloucestershire Regiment, won his VC at Boiselle in France on 2/3 July for most conspicuous bravery, coolness and determination during severe operations of a prolonged nature. He was thirty-six at the time. He had been educated at the Oratory School, Edgbaston, and Balliol College, Oxford. At the outbreak of the South African War in 1899 he enlisted as a private in the Middlesex Yeomanry and served throughout that war, in which he was twice wounded. He lost an eye in operations with the Somaliland Camel Force in 1914–15 when he was mentioned in despatches and awarded the DSO.

In the operations in France and Belgium in 1915–16 he had been severely wounded several times and had lost his left hand. In spite of these disabilities, he commanded the 8th Battalion of the Gloucesters, which took La Boiselle. It was owing in great measure to his dauntless courage and inspiration that a serious reverse was averted. After three other battalion commanders had become casualties he controlled their commands and ensured that the ground gained was held at all costs. In organising the positions to be held he exposed himself fearlessly and appeared to bear a charmed life.

He was wounded no less than eight times during the 1914–18 War in which, in addition to the VC, he was awarded the CB, the CMG, the Croix d'Officier de l'Ordre de la Couronne and the Croix de Guerre. The fabulous figure with the black patch over the missing eye and the empty sleeve pinned across his chest, the bristling little moustache and the long row of medals, the impeccably turned out, erect, small figure, slim and hard as nails, was an inspiration to be with. No day was ever too long for him, no mission too dangerous, no obstacle too big. He had even plucked out his wounded eye himself when he found it was no longer of service to him. Truly this man's spirit burned like a flame in his battered body.

Brevet-Major William La Touche Congreve of the Rifle Brigade won his VC in France between 6 and 20 July. He was the son of Lieut-General Sir Walter Congreve who, as a captain in the Rifle Brigade, had won the VC in the South African War on 15 December 1899. This was the second instance of a father and son winning the Victoria Cross—the first being Lord Roberts and his son. And in both cases the son was killed in winning his Cross.

During the operations in France and Belgium Major La Touche Congreve had been awarded the DSO, the MC and the Legion of Honour. During the fourteen days of July preceding his death he had constantly inspired those around him by numerous acts of gallantry. As Brigade Major he not only conducted battalions personally up to their positions but, despite the fact that he was suffering severely from the effects of gas and heavy shelling, he showed supreme courage in assisting the Medical Officer at his brigade headquarters to remove the wounded to places of safety. He was finally shot and killed instantly. He was buried at Corbie on the Somme, and his father, who was then commanding a corps in France, attended his funeral.

On 9 August a very memorable VC was gained at Guillemont in France by Captain Noel Godfrey Chavasse, MC, of the Royal Army Medical Corps (attached to 1/10th Battalion Liverpool Regiment Territorial Force). During an attack he tended the wounded all day under heavy fire and through the following night. Next day he took a stretcher-bearer up to the advanced trenches and, under murderous shell-fire, carried an urgent case for 500yds to safety, being wounded by a shell splinter in the side during the journey. Altogether he saved the lives of some twenty wounded men, besides the cases which passed through his hands as a medical officer. Within a year Captain Chavasse was awarded a bar to his VC in Belgium for equally courageous rescue work which he carried on unceasingly despite the fact that he had been severely wounded earlier in the action. This very gallant officer died of his wounds and his bar was awarded posthumously. This was one of the only three bars to the VC that have ever been given, the others being to Lieutenant A. Martin-Leake, RAMC, and Captain C. H. Upham, New Zealand Military Forces (in the Second World War).

Private John Chipman Kerr (generally known as 'Chip') of the 49th Battalion Canadian Infantry won his VC on 16 September. The 49th Battalion took part in the great Canadian attack which moved irresistibly forward. However, the advance had been held up on the evening of the 15th by a section of German trench which was being resolutely defended. On the afternoon of the 16th a party of bombers from the 49th Battalion undertook to clear this difficult obstacle. Private Kerr, who was acting as first bayonet-man, moved forward in advance of the party. A grenade was thrown at him which blew off the upper joint of his right fore-finger and wounded him in the right side. By this time the other members of the assaulting party had closed up with him. Their bombs failed to shift the defenders. So Kerr climbed out of the trench in full view of the enemy and moved along the parados. Despite loss of blood he had still clung to his rifle and two grenades and was full of fight. He tossed the grenades into the enemy trench and opened fire with his rifle. He then jumped down into the enemy trench with the remainder of the party at his heels. The enemy, thinking they were surrounded, put up their hands and surrendered. The official recommendation said: 'The action of Private Kerr at this juncture resulted in the capture of 62 prisoners and 250 yards of trench.'

Lieutenant (Temporary Lieut-Colonel) Roland Boys Bradford, MC, 9th Battalion Durham Light Infantry, won his VC on 1 October 1916 at Eaucourt d'Abbaye (France). At twenty-four he was very young to be commanding a battalion. He was educated at the Royal Naval School, Eltham, as were his brothers, Captain T. A. Bradford, DSO, and Lieutenant G. N. Bradford, VC, RN, who won his Cross at Zeebrugge (Belgium) on the night of 22/23

April 1918. The Bradford family was the fourth, and last, example of two brothers winning the Victoria Cross. In the British attack on 1 October 1916 Boys Bradford's battalion was in support. One of the leading battalions, with its commanding officer wounded and its flanks dangerously exposed, was in a critical position. At the urgent request of its CO, Lieut-Colonel Bradford took command of his battalion as well as his own. By his fearless energy and skilful leadership of both battalions, Bradford succeeded in rallying the attack and they captured their objectives. He afterwards became a brigadier-general and was killed in action in November 1917.

One of the greatest British battle leaders of the century, who finished the First World War as a brigadier, VC, CMG, DSO and two bars, with a brevet-majority, brevet-lieut-colonelcy and six mentions in despatches, and who had been wounded nine times, was Bernard Freyberg. His father was a New Zealander, though he himself was born in London on 21 March 1889. In November 1909 Bernard Freyberg was commissioned as a second lieutenant in the 6th Hauraki Regiment, New Zealand Military Forces, and later transferred to the British Regular Army. He was a company commander in the Hood Battalion of the Royal Naval Division in 1914 and 1915 and from 1915 to 1917 commanded the Hood Battalion. He took part in the operations on the Gallipoli peninsula from the landing until the evacuation. On the night of 24/25 April 1915 he won a very gallant DSO when he swam ashore at night, alone, and lit flares on the beach to distract attention from the landing operations which were taking place elsewhere. He was several hours in the water before being picked up.

Freyberg was then transferred to France and there took part in the battles of the Somme (1916), the Ancre (1916), Arras (1917), Bullecourt (1917), the third battle of Ypres, Passchendaele (1917–18), the first battle of the Lys and of the Forest of Nieppe (1918), the battle of Hill 63 and Ploegsteert Wood, the fourth battle of Ypres, Gheluvelt, the battle of Ledingham, the second battle of Lys and the crossings of the Scheldt and Dendre! He was awarded the Victoria Cross on 13 November 1916 while commanding the Hood Battalion as a captain (temporary lieut-colonel) for his brave and brilliant leading of his battalion. He carried the initial attack straight through the German front-line system of trenches, by which time the battalion had become much disorganised. He then personally rallied and re-formed them, with men of various other units, and led them on to the successful assault of the second objective, capturing many prisoners. During this advance he was twice wounded but remained in command and held his very advanced position for the remainder of the day and throughout the night. When reinforced next morning he organised the attack on a strongly fortified village and personally led the assault, capturing the village and 500 prisoners. In this operation he was again wounded.

Later in the afternoon Freyberg was wounded once more, this time severely, but he refused to leave the line until he had issued final instructions. His fearless and inspired leadership enabled the lodgement in the most advanced objective to be permanently held, and on this strong-point the line was eventually formed.

Wherever the fighting was thickest Freyberg was always to be found leading and encouraging his troops. He gained a second bar to his DSO in the last five minutes of the war. In an action at Lessines he led the cavalry in a dash to save the bridge over the river Dendre, and with nine men only he rushed a village on horseback and captured 104 prisoners two minutes before the Armistice began. He was a man of fine physique, a great swimmer, a keen yachtsman, and a good Rugby player. To his men he appeared indomitable and indestructible. In the Second World War he greatly distinguished himself in command of the New Zealand Division and won a third bar to his DSO. He was created a KCB and KBE, was Governor-General of New Zealand from 1946 to 1952, and was created a baron in 1951.

It was not until November 1916 that at long last the Somme battle was over. Then the controversy started as to whether it had been worth while. The casualties were appalling (British 343,112, French 143,072) and Winston Churchill was very critical indeed. But some experts believed the German casualties to be even higher. Certainly the Somme achieved its first objective of relieving pressure on the French; and as the German Chief of Staff, General Ludendorff, declared that the German Army had been fought to a standstill by the end of 1916, it could be argued that the Somme paved the way to final victory. But the criticism against Haig and Robertson was severe. Why hadn't the attack been stopped when it was obvious that no breakthrough could be effected? This, and other, questions were not easy to answer.

Meanwhile Kitchener was dead, drowned when the cruiser *Hampshire* struck a mine off the Orkneys on the way to Russia on 6 June. His death came as a great shock to the British people, to whom he was a legend and a tower of strength, although he had actually long passed the zenith of his physical and mental powers. On 7 December Lloyd George replaced Asquith as prime minister. Haig had already met and disliked Lloyd George when the latter had become Secretary of State for War in the summer of 1916. He was now to be thrown into the closest relationship with him.

CHAPTER NINE

The 1917 Offensive: Passchendaele, Cambrai

The Allied plan on the Western Front had been agreed by Haig
and Joffre at the Conference of Chantilly in November 1916,
where the main conclusion reached had been that France should
be the main theatre of war and that a new offensive should be
mounted there not later than mid-February 1917. All the chief
ministers attending the conference were satisfied with these
conclusions, except for Lloyd George, who was utterly opposed
to the hard slog with its accompanying ghastly casualties—and
there was a widespread feeling inside and outside Parliament that
he was right. However, M. Briand, the French prime minister,
bowing to the French people's disapproval of the way the war
was being conducted, decided to make a change in the High
Command. General Joffre, who had reigned supreme for three
years, was made a Marshal of France and retired; and General
Nivelle was made commander-in-chief in his place over the heads
of Foch, Pétain and de Castelnau. Nivelle was a good talker and
he quite captivated Briand and Lloyd George.

This change was at once followed by a change of plan. Nivelle
wished the new offensive to be undertaken principally by the
French armies and to be launched across the river Aisne—much
further south than had been arranged at Chantilly. The British
role was to make a subsidiary attack on Vimy Ridge. This change
of plan meant the postponement of the offensive until April.

Lloyd George was generally hostile to another large-scale offensive in the west, but at least Nivelle's plan was preferable from his point of view to the Haig–Joffre plan, which would have committed the British Army to another major battle. Lloyd George, however, saw in the new command set-up in France an opportunity of diminishing the power of the British Army leaders— particularly Haig and Robertson. There is no doubt that Kitchener, Robertson and Haig between them had exercised far greater powers over the general direction of the war, *vis-à-vis* the Government, than any British generals did in the Second World War. In that war Winston Churchill was generally saying: 'On, on the noble English', while the generals were advising that less haste would make for more speed. In the First World War it was the other way round.

The Conference of Calais on 26 February 1917 was one of the most remarkable events of the First World War. It was convened ostensibly to discuss problems of transport. No hint was given either to Haig or to Robertson that any question of command was even under consideration. At a conference that Lloyd George had with the French prime minister and General Nivelle it was agreed that Nivelle should become supreme commander of the French and British armies with a British chief of staff, General Sir Henry Wilson. This decision was confirmed on 24 February at a meeting of the War Cabinet and again by the Conference of Calais on the 26th. Haig and Robertson, as is made clear in Haig's diary and in Robertson's memoirs, were horrified and furious when they heard afterwards of these decisions and protested vehemently to Lloyd George. And of course Haig protested to the king, who had heard nothing about it at all. Haig was particularly enraged at any idea of his *bête noire*, Henry Wilson, being in any position of authority over him. He was also put out at being placed under the command of an untried French general, who was much junior to himself—which was quite understandable.

Eventually Lloyd George agreed to a modification of the proposals, which were then confined to the period of the forthcoming offensive only—and even for that period gave Haig the right of appeal to the British Cabinet if he considered that the safety of his troops was endangered by Nivelle's orders. There was in fact nothing particularly wrong with the idea of a supreme commander being appointed over both the national commanders-in-chief, as Foch was in 1918 and Eisenhower was in 1944. But it was clearly wrong that one national C-in-C should be in charge of both his own and his ally's army. It was the way the whole matter was done that so deeply offended both Haig and Robertson, and they never forgave or trusted Lloyd George again.

Winston Churchill, in like circumstances, would have removed Haig as he did Dill, Wavell and Auchinleck in the Second World War, but Lloyd George depended on Unionist support in the House of Commons and the Unionists were basically strong supporters of Robertson and Haig, though many of them were shaken by the enormous casualties suffered by the British Army for such poor visible results. Lloyd George did not dare to remove these two generals, but he was determined to assert his authority as prime minister to limit their powers.

However, for the moment Lloyd George was defeated by events. Nivelle's offensive, launched on 16 April, was a complete débâcle. A wave of criticism and resentment swept over France. There were very serious mutinies in the French Army and Haig had even more reason for being alarmed that French morale might collapse. On 15 May Nivelle was dismissed and General Pétain was appointed in his place. He was determined that the French Army should not be committed to any further major offensive operations for the time being.

Major-General Sir Edward Spears, who was the British liaison officer with the French in both world wars, was full of praise for General Pétain for his action in dealing with the mutinies in the French Army. He says (*Two Men who Saved France*): 'Not only did Pétain save the French Army, but also France and England.' Field-Marshal Lord Gort said:

In 1917 General Philippe Pétain was selected to deal with the situation. It is to his enduring fame, which his actions in the Second World War can never erase, that he saved France and the Allied cause by his handling of the crisis which followed

General Nivelle's departure. His firm leadership and his personal visits to mutinous units of the French Army restored confidence in a surprisingly short time.

(J. R. Colville, *Man of Valour*)

The remainder of 1917 was occupied by the great British offensive in Flanders which came to be known as Passchendaele. No other battle in Haig's career caused such bitter controversy as this one. The enormous losses sustained and the appalling conditions in which the battle was fought combined to give ammunition to his critics. Lloyd George says in his *War Memoirs*, Vol IV (p 2110 ff):

And now we come to Passchendaele, the campaign in the mud, which, with the Somme and Verdun will always rank as the most glorious, tenacious, grim, futile and bloody fights ever waged in the history of war. Each of these battles lasted for months. None of them attained the objective for which they were fought. In each case it was obvious early in the struggle to everyone who watched its course—except to those who were responsible for the strategic plan that wrought the grisly tragedy—that the goal would not be reached. Taken together they were responsible for the slaughter or mutilation of between 2,000,000 and 3,000,000 brave men. The tale of these battles constitutes a trilogy illustrating the unquenchable heroism that will never accept defeat and the inexhaustible vanity that will never admit a mistake.

By this time the Flying Corps had grown enormously and played a major role in the operations. Lieutenant (Temporary Captain) Albert Ball, of the 7th Battalion Notts and Derby Regiment (Sherwood Foresters) and Royal Flying Corps, was awarded a posthumous VC for flying services in France between 25 April and 6 May 1917. The official citation records:

In this period Captain Ball took part in 26 combats in the air and destroyed 11 hostile aeroplanes, drove down two out of control and forced several to land. In these combats Captain Ball, flying alone, on one occasion fought six hostile machines, twice he fought five and once four. When leading two other British aeroplanes he attacked an enemy formation of eight. On each of these occasions he brought down at least one enemy. Several times his aeroplane was badly damaged, once so seriously that, but for the most delicate handling, his machine would have collapsed as nearly all the control wires had been shot away. On returning with a damaged machine he had always to be restrained from immediately going up in another. In all Captain Ball has destroyed 43 German aeroplanes and one balloon, and has always displayed most exceptional courage, determination and skill.

Forty-three German planes destroyed is likely to be a considerable under-estimate as Captain Ball was always rather reluctant to claim any but those which were seen to be completely destroyed. He was certainly one of the most remarkable and intrepid young airmen of all time and when he was killed at the age of twenty he had won more honours for bravery in action than any man of his age had ever achieved before. He was the first officer to receive the DSO three times, and his full awards for gallantry were the Victoria Cross, the Military Cross, the Russian Order of St George and the Legion of Honour. He was mentioned in despatches many times and also referred to in Parliament. On his twentieth birthday he was presented with the honorary freedom of his native city, Nottingham.

Albert Ball joined up at the outbreak of war as a private in the 2/7th Sherwood Foresters. But he was mad keen on flying and took every opportunity to do so. He was religiously minded and was a young man of the highest ideals and principles; he became a dedicated fighter pilot. He fought for his home and country and he fought always with a song in his heart—and death in his hands. 'I always sing', he once said, 'when I am up in the clouds. I am never afraid. I am looked after by God.'

Ball was indeed utterly fearless and imbued with only one idea— to engage the enemy in the air at any place, at any time and against any odds. During the early battles on the Somme he would often be up in the air at 2.30 am, long before daylight, and keep flying until 9.30 at night. Although completely confident in himself he was a man of absolute humility and never sought stardom. In ordinary life he was a quiet and retiring man—but in the air he was a killer. However, he was never reckless. He took immense trouble to make himself an efficient airman and a crack shot. He kept himself, his gun and his plane in perfect order. He himself was always superbly fit in mind and body—because he knew he had to be to keep at the top. From the time he joined the Royal Flying Corps until his death he spent most of his waking hours scanning the skies for enemy aircraft, and although his flying life was a very short one—and his RFC service amounted in all to about one year—he certainly lived a lifetime in that year and died as he would have wished—engaging superior numbers of the enemy.

Ball was awarded the MC in the early summer of 1916 and his first DSO in September of the same year. He was then promoted lieutenant and was almost immediately awarded a bar to his DSO. He was immediately promoted captain and, in November 1916, received the second bar to his DSO. And with all these honours poured upon him he remained as unaffected and unconceited as he had always been. In all, he was engaged in over 100 air combats and the precise number of enemy aircraft he shot down must remain somewhat problematical. Finally he was reported missing on 8 May 1917. It was afterwards discovered that his plane had crashed near the village of Annoeullin on 6 May. The villagers said that he had attacked three German machines, shot down two and driven the third away. He was by that time flying very low and was brought down by anti-aircraft fire. The Germans buried him in the German cemetery at Annoeullin with the greatest respect and honour. Then, at the risk of death, a German pilot crossed the lines to drop a cylinder reporting his death. There was a great cameraderie between the top air aces of Germany and Britain in the First World War. After the war the 207th Squadron RFC erected a beautiful cross on his grave.

General Sir Hugh Trenchard, the head of the Royal Flying

Corps and later Marshal of the RAF, writing to Ball's father on 8 May 1917, said:

> He was the most daring, skilful and successful pilot the Royal Flying Corps has ever had. Everyone in the Corps looked upon him as their own personal asset and he was a most popular officer. His good spirits were infectious and, whatever squadron he was with, the officers of it tried to work up to his level and reputation. I have never met a man who has been so successful as he was in such a short time and one who was so modest and reliable.

And Sir Douglas Haig wrote:

> By his unrivalled courage and brilliant ability as an airman, Captain Ball won for himself a prominent place in a most gallant Service. His loss was a great one but the splendid spirit which he typified, and did so much to foster, lives after him. The record of his deeds will ever stir the pride and imagination of his countrymen and act as an example and incentive to those who have taken up his work.

Captain Ball was a typical example of leadership by example, and the example he set was quite invaluable to all his contemporaries.

The fierce battles in France in the second half of 1917, which were generally known as third Ypres or Passchendaele, were fought in appalling conditions of rain and mud, which caused intense hardship to the troops concerned. No less than fourteen Victoria Crosses were gained on 31 July, the first day of the battle of Ypres, including the bar to his VC won by Captain N. G. Chavasse, RAMC, at Wieltje.

Lloyd George considered that we should husband our resources of men and munitions in 1917 with a view to launching a decisive blow in 1918 when the Americans were coming into the war. Haig, on the other hand, considered that relaxation of pressure would be fatal and would give the Germans time to recover.

Moreover, he considered that to remain on the defensive would have a depressing effect on our armies in the field and lower the already shaky morale of the French people and the French Army.

Winston Churchill said: 'The new offensive planned by Haig and Robertson confused the issue, darkened counsel, numbed misgivings, overpowered the dictates of prudence and cleared the way for a forlorn expenditure of valour and life without equal in futility.' But Winston makes it clear that Haig and Robertson had several supporters in the Cabinet and 'in the end the P.M. did not feel strong enough to face the Haig–Robertson combination. He submitted with resentful fatalism'. (*The World Crisis 1916–18*, Part 2.)

Certainly the total cost of the battle was appalling—a quarter of a million casualties for an average gain of four miles. Passchendaele—above all, the last phase—was the ultimate in horror on the battlefield. However, on the credit side Passchendaele made any German attempt to exploit the weakness of the French Army impossible and, as far as could be ascertained, the Germans suffered as many casualties in the battle as the British. Haig claimed that, as a result of the battle, the German Army was as good as finished.

Coming events proved this claim to be quite untrue. By the end of the year German divisions were flowing back from Russia, sufficient to make good the damage of 1917 and to accumulate a striking force for the Spring of 1918. But the Germans afterwards admitted that the losses they sustained in France in 1917 contributed directly to their failure to win the war in the following March and April.

Unhappily the Cambrai battle which followed brought no lessening of the criticism of Robertson and Haig, despite its brilliant start. The offensive was entrusted to Byng's 3rd Army and embodied tactics of a revolutionary kind. Instead of the long preliminary bombardment to cut the enemy wire, 300 British tanks achieved complete surprise by advancing out of the early morning mist on 20 November. Massive artillery fire was put down in front of the tanks as soon as they were well on their way. The tanks crushed the wire, dropping fascines of brushwood into the trenches which they then crossed, followed by the infantry. The advance went wonderfully well. Generally speaking, it breached the German defences on a six-mile front.

However, by that time the tanks had all come to a standstill and their crews were exhausted. The Germans, as usual, were quick and bold in rushing up their reserves and halted any further advance by the infantry. Then, on 30 November, the Germans counter-attacked heavily and won back all the ground that the British had gained—and more. It must be remembered, however, that at the end of October the War Cabinet had ordered Haig to send five divisions to bolster up the Italian front.

It was unfortunate—but perhaps only natural—that the initial British success at Cambrai was trumpeted abroad very loudly— and the subsequent reverse was only very slowly and very grudgingly released.

Lloyd George was of the opinion that the losses the British had sustained at Passchendaele were directly responsible for our failure to make a decisive success of Cambrai. He wrote:

Cambrai was the only complete surprise the British Army had contrived to inflict upon the Germans. Their strongest defences had been broken through. For the first time we had reached the open country behind their lines. Had there been adequate reserves to throw in, Cambrai would have been captured, the German defence system would have been dislocated, a new retirement would have been imposed on the enemy, and the time and strength devoted to prepare his March offensive against our lines would have had to be spent in reorganising his own defences. One-fourth of the men flung away so profligately at Passchendaele would have sufficed to win this signal victory and to exploit it.

The Cabinet was also very critical of the way so complete a reverse had been so very tardily reported, whereas news of any success reached them in a few hours. Lloyd George himself severely criticised 'these repeated offensives' which had meant that out of the sixty-four British divisions in France fifty-seven had already

been thrown into the battle. He expressed himself fully in favour
of 'General Pétain's policy of limited offensives'. Or, in other
words, the policy advocated by General Rawlinson after Neuve
Chapelle of 'bite and hold'.

CHAPTER TEN

Lloyd George and the Generals: the Supreme War Council

Lloyd George was now in a dilemma. He did not dare to dismiss his official military advisers, although he profoundly distrusted the advice they gave him. He therefore decided to set up an inter-allied body to co-ordinate the war strategy as a whole. At the Conference of Rapallo in November 1917, he and Painlevé, the French premier, agreed to set up the Inter-Allied Supreme War Council at Versailles, and Lloyd George appointed Sir Henry Wilson to it as British military representative. Wilson was an ardent believer in the superiority of French generalship and was a close friend of Foch, who was appointed as the French military representative.

Lloyd George put his proposals before the War Cabinet in London and the House of Commons and obtained the approval of Parliament for his action. He was also able to announce the backing of President Wilson as well. On 30 November 1917 the Supreme War Council assembled at Versailles. It was a complete triumph for Lloyd George which was entirely due to his determination and will-power and the extremely clever way in which he handled the matter.

In France the initiative had passed to the Germans. Russia had ceased to play any part in the war and German reinforcements from the eastern front were pouring into France and Belgium. The British Army was now 100,000 under strength. The question whether the Germans would take advantage of this situation to stage a major offensive in the New Year was occupying the minds of all those in positions of authority, both political and military. It was now that the bad relations between Lloyd George and his generals bore such bitter fruit. For the last two years he had been seeing thousands of men slaughtered in battles of which he had entirely disapproved and he and his War Cabinet were in consequence not prepared to give high priority to the manpower demands of the Western Front. The Prime Minister's feelings were understandable but they had tragic results which nearly enabled the Germans to win the war.

In the early months of 1918 the future of the campaign in Palestine was the subject of high debate in the councils of the Allies. Lloyd George had always believed that the shortest road to victory did not lie in the western theatre but in eliminating Germany's lesser allies in the subsidiary theatres. Despite the fact that the Turks had been heavily defeated and Jerusalem captured, Lloyd George demanded a further offensive in Palestine for 1918, directed at driving Turkey out of the war altogether, and he wished to supply Allenby with sufficient men and material to enable him to reach Damascus and if possible Aleppo. The Prime Minister was supported on the military side by Sir Henry Wilson. He was opposed by the Chief of the Imperial General Staff, Sir William Robertson, and the Commander-in-Chief in France, Sir Douglas Haig. These two maintained that defeat in France would inevitably mean the loss of the war, whereas the capture of Damascus and Aleppo could have little real effect. The Egyptian Expeditionary Force, if it remained on the defensive, could spare two divisions to strengthen the Western Front and much shipping and other resources could be saved by calling a halt to what was a side issue compared with the vital one which was now facing Britain in France.

But Lloyd George had his way, and at a meeting of the Supreme War Council held at the end of January his plan for a decisive offensive against Turkey in the Spring of 1918 was endorsed. But another two divisions might have made all the difference on that fatal morning of 21 March 1918, in France. Winston Churchill, although he interfered perhaps more than he should have done in military matters in the Second World War, seldom thought of overruling his leading military advisers on a matter of major military importance. But Winston's long-term appreciation of Allied world strategy was masterly.

In his *World Crisis*, Vol III, *1916–1918*, which was of course written after the war, Churchill has a remarkable chapter which he called 'The Blood Test'. In this he seeks to prove, with considerable foundation, that Robertson and Haig were wrong in maintaining that their big offensives, such as the Somme, Passchendaele and Cambrai, though appallingly costly in British lives, were conducive to the wearing down of the German Army on the Western Front which resulted in final victory. In all the big Allied offensives we suffered greater losses than the Germans and, as for morale, our offensives had not weakened that of the German Army as was proved by the tremendous drive and spirit they produced in March 1918. Winston maintained that it was Ludendorff who lost the war for Germany by his great offensives in the first half of 1918. 'The climax of the German effort was reached in July' he wrote. 'Ludendorff had worn out his army in the grand manner, but thoroughly, and the Allied offensive then began.'

One has to read Haig's diaries to realise that he had not a high opinion of Winston Churchill—and this was reciprocated in some degree. Not that Winston did not have a high opinion of Haig personally. He certainly had, but he had no opinion of his strategy, which Winston maintained was merely 'killing Germans in a war of attrition' (*World Crisis*, Vol III, p 46). Winston was equally critical of Robertson,

whose policy was a succession of frontal assaults upon fortified positions, defended by barbed wire and machine guns without the necessary superiority in numbers, or an adequate artillery, or any novel offensive method. He succeeded in enforcing this policy against the better judgement of successive Cabinets or War Councils with the result that when he left the War Office in February 1918, the British and French Armies were at their weakest point in strength and fighting power and the Germans for the first time since the original invasion had gathered a great superiority of reserves as to be able to launch a gigantic attack.

Churchill is particularly critical of Robertson over the blood-bath of Passchendaele. 'Undeterred by the fact that there was then no hope of getting a decision he proceeded to drive the unfortunate ministers to authorise its prolongation into the depths of winter.'

Winston poses to himself, and to his readers, the question: How, then, should the war on the Western Front have been waged? He mentions that there were five Allied offensives—one of them the first day of the battle of Cambrai—which opened brilliantly and would have been more costly in men to the Germans than to the Allies. The question was whether it was wise policy to seek to pursue prolonged offensives on the largest scale in order to wear down the enemy by attrition. If instead we could only have compelled the enemy to attack, might not our victory have come sooner? There, then, you have both sides of the argument.

On 16 February Lloyd George reported to the king his intention to dismiss Robertson. It was now a simple issue—Robertson or himself. If the king insisted on retaining his Chief of Staff then he—the Prime Minister—would have to resign. That afternoon the Government announced Robertson's resignation and Sir Henry Wilson's appointment in his place. Robertson was offered Wilson's place as Principal Military Representative at Versailles, but he refused and Rawlinson was appointed. Robertson had hoped that Haig would give in his own resignation; but he did nothing of the kind. He made it clear that he would abide by the decision of the War Cabinet.

Haig's main reason for not resigning was the one he had held all along, that he alone could bring victory on the Western Front. The Army was devoted to him and had as much faith in his leadership as ever. Moreover there was really no one who could take his place. He did not consider that it would be fair to the Army for them to have a new commander-in-chief at such a critical time. So Robertson's long tenure of power was over. He later became C-in-C Home Forces in place of Lord French and in 1919 handed over Home Forces to Haig and took up the last appointment of his military career as C-in-C British Army of the Rhine. Lloyd George, as prime ministers are apt to be, was ungenerous to those who opposed him. When the list of war honours was announced Robertson was well down the list with a baronetcy and the sum of £10,000. Haig got an earldom and £100,000; French and Allenby received £50,000 each and most of the army commanders (with the exception of Gough) £30,000 each. Wilson, Birdwood and Trenchard each received £10,000, the same as Robertson. However, Robertson was eventually made a field-marshal, thus becoming the first British soldier to rise from the ranks to that topmost rank in the Army. On 11 February 1933, after playing eighteen holes of golf the previous day, he died of a thrombosis, aged 73. He had rendered wonderful service to the Army and to his country.

From every battlefield there have been inspiring stories of spiritual leadership by Army chaplains.* In the First World War there were the fabulous Geoffrey Studdert-Kennedy, more commonly known as 'Woodbine Willie', and Tubby Clayton of Toc H; and the padré VCs, the Rev E. N. Mellish, the Rev W. R. F. Addison and the Rev T. B. Hardy.

Studdert-Kennedy was one of the most remarkable war chaplains of the First World War—or any other war. So great a man as William Temple, later Archbishop of Canterbury, considered him to be, in his capacity to move men's hearts, the finest priest he had ever come across. And as a mover of men's hearts William Temple himself was very hard to beat. In appearance Studdert-Kennedy was insignificant; small, with bat ears, large brown eyes and generally untidily dressed. He could swear like a trooper—and often did—and was anathema to many orthodox general officers in the Army. For much of his life he was afflicted with asthma and he eventually worked himself into an early

---

* I have written at length about the chaplains in my book, *In This Sign Conquer: The Story of the Army Chaplains.*

grave. But his courage shone like a flame and he would never give in. He was awarded the MC for gallantry at Messines in 1917. He was essentially a front-line padré and, much as he often hated it, he felt he had to go where his men went. Before a trench raid he would hold services for the men who were to undertake it, gathered round him in their tin hats and with blackened faces. He didn't have to suggest a service—the men did, and it strengthened the bonds between them enormously.

When he first came to France the Rev Theodore Bayley Hardy —afterwards the Rev T. B. Hardy, VC, DSO, MC, the most decorated of all war-time chaplains—asked Studdert-Kennedy the best way of working. The latter replied:

Live with the men, go everywhere they go. Make up your mind you will share their risks, and more, if you can do any good. The line is the key to the whole business. Work in the very front and they will listen to you; but if you stay behind you are wasting your time. Men will forgive you anything but lack of courage and devotion.

Studdert-Kennedy was a very robust Christian. He wrote a lot of poetry and very down-to-earth stuff it was. In the following lines from his poem, 'Suffering God', are to be found the key to his whole philosophy of life:

Peace does not mean the end of all our striving;
Joy does not mean the drying of our tears;
Peace is the power that comes to souls arriving
Up to the light where God himself appears.

He was an intense thinker and a merciless dissector and analyser of his own thoughts. He discovered that a great deal of prayer in peace and war was for survival. He condemned this and said that true prayer was for courage to endure, never for permission to survive.

It was in April 1918 that the Rev T. B. Hardy became the fourth padré in our history to win the Victoria Cross. He was attached to the 8th Battalion the Lincolnshire Regiment. The act of gallantry took place near Bucquoy, east of Gommecourt in France. He had already been awarded the DSO in September 1917 and the MC a month later. He followed the advice given to him by Studdert-Kennedy to the letter. He won his VC when he went out with a patrol 400yd beyond our front line to succour a wounded officer. He remained with him until assistance could be obtained to bring him in. On three occasions he went out to tend the wounded in no-man's-land, quite regardless of his personal safety. Everyone knew that his end was inevitable and he was killed in action on 18 October 1918, only three months after his award of the VC had been gazetted.

The Commanding Officer of the 8th Lincolns wrote to a member of Hardy's family:

He appealed to us all, both officers and men, by his absolute fearlessness, physical and moral, and by his simple sincerity and lack of cant or humbug. We loved him for his self-effacing devotion to duty. His gallantry in action won him distinction which will make his name famous in history and yet his retiring nature made it almost a penance to wear those ribbons which most of us would give our right arm for. What his loss has meant to us is more than I can ever express.

That is what leadership is all about.

CHAPTER ELEVEN

The German Offensive of March 1918

All Haig's information was to the effect that the Germans would stage a major offensive sometime in March 1918; and on the 21st the long-expected attack began. Its purpose was to drive a wedge between the British and French armies; accordingly the main onslaught was directed against General Gough's 5th Army on the extreme right of the British line. This army held a front of forty-two miles, from just south of Barisis to a little north of Gouzecourt (ten miles south-west of Cambrai). For the defence of this long line, Gough had twelve divisions and three cavalry divisions.

The 3rd Army, under General Byng, held a front of twenty-eight miles, from the left front of the 5th Army to near Gavrelle (six miles north-east of Arras). Byng had at his disposal fourteen divisions. Thus, with a much shorter front, he had two more divisions than Gough.

For the defence of the next thirty-three miles from Gavrelle to Armentières, both inclusive, the 1st Army had fourteen (including two Portuguese) divisions. The 2nd Army had twelve divisions for the occupation of a front of twenty-three miles.

When this number of troops had been allotted to armies by Haig, there remained only eight divisions for the GHQ reserve. These eight divisions were distributed behind the 126-mile-long British front, two behind each army. The smallness of the reserves was very disquieting. Besides the GHQ reserves certain divisions were held in reserve by the armies and corps. Out of a total of 99 divisions, exclusive of cavalry and American troops, the French had 60 in the line and 39 in reserve. When the German offensive began there were 1,144 British aircraft available. In the areas of the 3rd and 5th Armies there were 579 serviceable aeroplanes, of which 261 were single-seater fighters. With the 1st and 2nd Armies there were about 400 machines, almost equally divided between them. Opposed to them there were 730 German aeroplanes, of which 326 were single-seater fighters. For the first time the German air concentration for a battle on the Western Front was greater than that of the Royal Flying Corps. The British had 12 battalions of tanks, 36 per battalion. To the 5th Army, three battalions were allotted; to the 3rd, four; and to the 1st, two. The remainder were in GHQ reserve.

As regards the terrain, the area, except for the devastated portions, was very open and unfenced. It had been under cultivation. The area devastated by the Germans in 1917, extending for many miles behind the front of the 5th and 3rd Armies, still presented a scene of utter devastation. Towns had been gutted; the villages were in ruins; trees and orchards had been cut down and only three or four feet of their trunks stood, dead and bare. The ground was intersected by old trenches, pitted with shell craters and obstructed by wire to a degree which made movement across country, even on foot, difficult and exhausting.

In spite of their failure on the Yser and before Ypres in October–November 1914, the German General Staff had never abandoned hope of breaking the Allied front in the West and thereby bringing about a decision. In the OHL (German Supreme Headquarters) appreciation dated 23 October 1917 it is stated: 'The guiding principle of our general military situation remains for the future as in the past that the decision lies in the Western Theatre of War.'

But until the success of the offensive in Italy was assured and it became certain that the French and British would send divisions to the Italian front, and that Russia would be out of the war, Ludendorff did not give the final decision for the great offensive in the West. It was not until 11 November 1917 that he summoned the chiefs of staff of the German Armies to a conference at Mons. Mark these fatal dates and places for Germany: 11 November, Armistice Day, when the war ended, and Mons where it all began four years earlier. At this conference the approximate date, February or March 1918, for the start of the operations was fixed and all the plans put in train. It is also interesting to note that these vital decisions were taken by the German general staff without the slightest reference to or interference from the government in Berlin (Edmonds, *Military Operations in France and Belgium 1918*, p 138). There is no doubt that in such matters a military dictatorship has a great advantage over an alliance of two democratic nations where the politicians play such a major part and there is no overall supreme military commander. Haig, like his German opposing generals, was always entirely convinced that the decision must come in the Western Theatre. Ludendorff was also very clear that, although they might be expected to strike against the French, their intention was to strike a knockout blow against the British. He envisaged that their attack, centred on St-Quentin, would gain the Somme line Ham–Peronne from which, with the left flank resting on the Somme, they could roll up the British front.

From the beginning of November 1917 onwards the collection of ammunition and other material had been taken in hand and the transfer of troops from east to west and from Italy continued. By 21 March 1918 the Germans had massed 192 divisions in France and Belgium compared with the British 58 and the French 99, giving the Germans an advantage of 35. A thorough course of intensive training for all German troops had been ordered and 58 divisions and a very large force of artillery were put through a special course of training in open warfare operations.

All this made rather a nonsense of Haig's idea that the German Army had been fought to a standstill by the end of 1917. General Ludendorff was in charge of all the higher planning and direction of the grand offensive—and he was certainly one of the outstanding generals of the First World War. The attack was to be made by five armies, with the main thrust on either side of St-Quentin against the front held by the British 5th Army being initiated by the German 18th Army. The German offensive was intended to strike the British, whom they rightly estimated would be opposing them over the whole frontage of the attack. 'We must beat the British' was continuously emphasised. The four German armies making the assault were, from right to left, the 17th, 2nd, 18th and 7th. A total of 63 divisions were collected for the assault, some 43 divisions of the 18th and 2nd armies being massed opposite the 14 divisions of Gough's 5th Army; 19 divisions of the 17th Army were to assault Byng's 3rd Army of 14 divisions.

Supporting this massive assault were 950 field batteries; 701 heavy batteries; 55 super-heavy batteries; 3,532 trench mortars; 38 flights of protection duty aeroplanes; 39 pursuit flights and 5 bombing squadrons. It was a gigantic staff exercise to concentrate these vast forces and their supporting services in the battle area, and the Germans tackled it with their usual masterly efficiency. Every form of false rumour was spread around. Feints and demonstrations were staged and on the actual front of the attack infinite precautions were taken to conceal the immense concentration of troops. All important moves were made by night; the attacking divisions were kept well back and brought up only at the latest moment. The concentration of the air force was very carefully thought out; additional hangars were put up and wireless stations and aerodromes installed. Tremendous care was taken to conceal and camouflage the artillery emplacements. It was planned that a hurricane of shelling should descend upon the forward British infantry positions.

As far as the German infantry assault went, great emphasis was placed on maintaining the momentum of the attack. They were warned that the opening bombardment would do no more than compel the enemy to take cover and thus give an opportunity of surprising him. It would hamper the enemy but not annihilate him. Its effect therefore had value only if the infantry accepted the opportunity 'by keeping close behind the barrage regardless of shell splinters. A single enemy machine gun which survives the bombardment does more harm than any number of our own shell splinters' (Ludendorff's orders for the attack).

The ground mist, which had begun to rise about 5 pm on the

evening of 20 March over the whole area occupied by the British 5th and 3rd armies, developed steadily into a thick fog during the night. About 4.40 am on the 21st a terrific bombardment opened with a crash on the whole front of the 5th Army, on three-quarters of the 3rd Army and on part of the front of the 1st Army. It continued with full intensity for two hours and included much gas (lachrymatory) shell. General Arthur Percival, who was commanding the 7th Bedfords, recorded in his diary: 'Certainly 21st March 1918 was a day that no one in the 7th Bedfords who survived it will ever forget. The Great German Offensive started suddenly, in pitch darkness, with the biggest artillery barrage I had ever heard. Even when daylight came everything was shrouded in a thick mist.' So heavy was the fire that the air seemed to vibrate with shell bursts. Fortunately the wind was not altogether favourable for the use of gas by the enemy. The shelling was chiefly directed on artillery positions, divisional headquarters, telephone exchanges and railway stations. Targets had been marked down with great accuracy. Communications were smashed, many defended areas were rendered untenable and all the battery positions which had been in use were deluged with gas, which mingled with the fog into a nauseating effect.

The reply of the British artillery was immediate. Batteries fired on their night defensive lines, which was all they could do. Despite the fog and the gas the troops in the whole of the battle zone manned their battle stations quickly. At 9.40 am, the time of the German assault, the fog lifted a bit in places but remained dense on the right of the 5th Army until after midday. The main attack was directed against the four corps of the 5th Army, north of the Oise, and of 6 and 4 Corps of the 3rd Army. The British wire had been fairly effectively cut by the bombardment and the British front-line trenches had suffered very severely. The redoubts and defended areas further back had for the most part escaped serious damage; but the garrisons could not see to shoot until the attack was close upon them, nor could their signals for artillery support be observed. Even some of the brigade headquarters did not know of the attack until the German infantry were close upon them.

The leading waves of German infantry swept forward, leaving

the posts and redoubts in the forward zone to be dealt with by special parties. The combination of fog and gas had served to make the defence's careful fire plans of rifles, machine-guns and artillery ineffective. But full marks must be given to the German infantry for pushing forward everywhere with the greatest verve and determination. The British plan for co-operation between the Artillery and the Royal Flying Corps failed completely. The causes of the failure were chiefly the fog itself and the fog of war, which resulted from the severance of telephone communications and the breakdown of the artillery wireless.

On 22 March fierce fighting continued. The Germans were able to bring fresh troops into the field against the exhausted and depleted British forces. Fog once more assisted the attackers— particularly on the right of the 5th Army. At 8 pm Gough tele-phoned to Haig to say that parties of the enemy had penetrated his reserve line. Haig concurred in his falling back, defending the line of the Somme and holding the Peronne bridgehead. But when he visited Gough at his headquarters he was surprised to learn that his troops were behind the Somme and the Tortville.

Whatever criticism may have been levelled at Haig, no one can deny that in this, the greatest crisis of his life, his behaviour and his demeanour were perfect. He reacted with great energy both physically and mentally and remained absolutely cool and unperturbed. What more can one ask of a commander-in-chief in such circumstances?

Owing to the better visibility in the north the attack against the 3rd Army proved less successful than that against the 5th, which caused acute disappointment to Ludendorff. None the less, Haig considered that the position was growing increasingly serious. General Pétain visited Haig at 4 pm on the 23rd and arranged to place large reinforcements on his right, to operate in the Somme valley. Haig records in his diary of that day: 'Pétain seems most anxious to do all he can to support me and agrees that the only principle which should guide us is to keep our two armies in touch.'

But when the two commanders-in-chief met again next day, 24 March, at 11 pm, Haig recorded in his diary: 'Pétain struck me as being very much upset, almost unbalanced and most anxious.' Haig asked him to concentrate as large a force as possible at Amiens, behind the centre of the retreating 5th Army. Pétain said he was giving Fayolle all his available troops, which he was concentrating at Montdidier, ie, behind the extreme right flank of the 5th Army. Pétain had directed Fayolle, in the event of the German advance being pressed still further, to fall back to the south-west towards Beauvais in order to cover Paris. It was at once clear to Haig that this would separate the French from the British right flank and so allow the enemy to penetrate between the two armies. He says in his diary: 'I gathered from my talk with Pétain that he had recently attended a Cabinet meeting in Paris and that his orders from his Government are to cover Paris at all costs.'

Haig realised at once that some urgent action must be taken at the highest Allied level to prevent the French and British armies being forced apart. He hurried back to his headquarters, reported this contemplated change in French strategy to the CIGS and Secretary of State in London and asked them to come to France at once and to arrange that General Foch should be given supreme control of the Allied operations in France.

General Wilson arrived at 11 am on the 25th and Haig told him that he must be supported at once north of the Somme by twenty French divisions. At present the British Army was bearing the whole weight of the German attack single-handed. And he estimated that the Germans still had twenty-five more divisions in reserve.

On the battlefront the ground mist had cleared; but in spite of this advantage to the defence, and the arrival of some French divisions on the 3rd Army front, the barrier of the Somme was lost and the right of the 3rd Army was over four miles behind the left of the 5th. Tuesday 26 March was a day of big decisions. Haig held a conference at Doullens, behind the front of the 3rd Army, at 11 am with Plumer (2nd Army), Horne (1st) and Byng (3rd). The C-in-C impressed on them that the covering of Amiens was of the first importance to our cause and that they must hold on until French support was forthcoming.

Then, also at Doullens at 12 noon, the most important conference of the war took place between Poincaré (President of France), Clemenceau (Premier), Foch, Pétain, Lord Milner (Secretary of State for War), General Wilson (CIGS), Laurence (CGS to Haig) and Haig himself. It was first decided that Amiens must be covered at all costs and, at Haig's urgent request, Foch was appointed to co-ordinate the action of all the Allied armies on the Western Front. Haig recorded: 'Foch seemed sound and sensible but Pétain had a terrible look. He had the appearance of a Commander who was in a funk and has lost his nerve.' But Pétain at once cancelled his instructions to Fayolle and ordered him to cover Amiens and maintain liaison with Haig. He further arranged to reinforce Fayolle with ten more divisions and four regiments of heavy artillery. Haig's high speed and dynamic action had galvanised the high command and saved the situation.

On 26 March General Sir Henry Rawlinson was informed on the telephone by General Wilson about the Doullens meeting, that Gough was being sent home and that he, Rawlinson, was to reconstruct the remains of the 5th Army as the 4th Army. This was obviously a Wilson appointment as he and Rawlinson had always been great friends. But Britain had no better fighting general than Henry Rawlinson. Haig had spoken up for Gough and said that he had fought hard and could not be blamed. However, in such circumstances the Government considered that it was best to 'change the bowling'. Rawlinson also recorded that our casualties had already been 80,000—and we were very short of men.

The German intention was now clearly to capture Amiens, which would cut the British Army off from the Channel ports, as well as separating them from the French Army. It was a grim prospect.

On the 28th Clemenceau came to lunch with Rawlinson at his new headquarters. The latter records:

As he was bidding me goodbye I said, 'Eh bien, M. le President, je ferai mon possible.'

'Non mon General,' he answered, 'Il faut faire l'impossible.'

'Eh bien, M. le President, je le ferai.' And the old man went away quite happy.

The relations between Lloyd George and Haig were in no way improved by the March crisis. Lloyd George, in his *Memoirs* (Vol V, p 2851) blames Haig for his dispositions before the battle. He writes: 'Haig's action is unaccountable. History can recall many cases of men in great positions who have been known to do inexplicable things in a great emergency.' Haig, on the other hand, records in his diary of 30 March: 'L.G. seems a cur and when I am with him I cannot resist a feeling of distrust of him and his intentions.' But Lloyd George had the last word in his *War Memoirs* published in 1936, eight years after Haig's death (Vol V, p 2934 ff). Referring to Ludendorff's March offensive he writes:

The German Army had every advantage which good leadership could confer; the British Army was placed under every disadvantage in which bad leadership could land any troops. Although British GHQ knew the attack was coming the preparations for defence were of the most slipshod character . . . Most of our reserves were in and behind that part of the line which was the remotest from the battlefield. Although GHQ was warned three weeks in advance that the greatest concentration of the enemy was opposite the weakest part of our line and that the shock would come there, it made no effort to strengthen it or to move any more of our reserves behind it.

Taking the whole front the opposing forces were substantially equal with a real mechanical superiority on the Allied side. But we so disposed our forces that for the first four days of the battle the enemy had an advantage of three or four to one in men and an even greater superiority in guns.

The official history tried to persuade us that Haig was right in keeping most of his Army as far away as possible from the area of the impending battle. It seems a novel theory that the further reinforcements are away from the fight the more useful they are when they are needed! That they are much more helpful when they are three days' journey from the battlefield than if they are only a few miles behind!

The final containment of the German offensive (which had cost the British 170,000 casualties), the plan for the concerted Allied counter-attack in which the British Army—particularly Rawlinson's 4th Army—played such a great part, and the masterly direction of Marshal Foch are all matters of history.

CHAPTER TWELVE

Foch, Supreme Commander
on the Western Front

Foch's appointment as Supreme Allied Commander on the Western Front was naturally a matter of particular satisfaction to Sir Henry Wilson, the British CIGS, who had made friends with Foch before the war, had collaborated with him on the role of the BEF in 1914, and had remained close to him ever since. Although Haig had been instrumental in getting Foch appointed Supreme Commander at a time of great crisis he was never an easy subordinate and was not slow to object to any order of Foch's with which he did not entirely agree. It was a measure of Foch's greatness that he handled Haig on such a loose rein, giving a little where necessary and using the power of the British Army to the full, but maintaining overall control in matters which he considered vital for the attainment of victory.

Lloyd George states in his *Memoirs* (Vol V, p 2925) that:

The arrangements for the co-ordination of the Higher Command on the Western Front concluded at Doullens on 26 March 1918 were finally re-worded to read as follows: 'General Foch is charged by the British, French and American Governments with the co-ordination of the action of the Allied Armies on the Western Front. To this end all powers necessary to secure effective realisation are conferred on him. The British, French and American Governments for this purpose entrust to General Foch the strategic direction of military operations. The Commanders-in-Chief of the British, French and American Armies have full control of the tactical employment of their forces. Each Commander-in-Chief will have the right of appeal to his Government if in his opinion the safety of his Army is compromised by any order received from General Foch.'

No one could discuss the generals of the present century without giving a very high place to Foch. Certainly no supreme commander ever had to assume control at such a critical moment, in the middle of a victorious offensive by the enemy. And it was certainly one of the most remarkable volte-faces in military history that, within the space of some six months, he had brought about the surrender of the German Army. Just as he would have been blamed if things had turned out otherwise, so he deserves the credit for his victorious generalship.

Foch was sixty-seven when he was appointed to his supreme command in 1918. But he was still immensely alert and vital, in both mind and body. He was in every sense a leader. He radiated confidence, strength and authority and was always ready and eager to accept responsibility, whatever the circumstances. He was a general who really looked the part—his large head bronzed and wrinkled, his heavy moustache grey and tobacco-stained, his piercing eyes, his mobile mouth, his short, square figure and his cavalry walk. Although he was no orator he was a vivid conversationalist and was fond of strong gesticulation to emphasise his points. No one could be dull or defeated in his company, because he never accepted the thought of defeat himself. As a tactician Foch may not have been so precise and scientific as Ludendorff and his remarkable team of staff officers, but as a strategist Foch was much more far-sighted. He never allowed his natural enthusiasm and optimism, and the imponderable magnetic qualities he possessed, to obscure the equilibrium of his mind, which remained cool and unaffected by danger, disappointment and defeat, and did not become unduly elated by success. On the other hand, he made the fullest use of his outstanding powers of leadership to influence events and people, and to retrieve a desperate situation which logic might have told him was irretrievable. And he did subscribe entirely to Napoleon's dictum: 'The moral is to the physical as three is to one.'

Foch came from a devout Catholic family and it is true to say that the strongest influences of his youth and his formative years were Napoleon Buonaparte and his Catholic faith. These beliefs illuminated his life, the flame burning brighter and fiercer as his future unfolded. From his childhood he pored over books about Napoleon and became dedicated to a military career. His piety, like his way of life, was simple, sincere and part of his nature. With it went his frugality and his pride in the fitness and keenness of his mind and body. He was no games player but a mountaineer, a sportsman and a fisherman. Above all he was a superb horseman; he loved horses and he always liked to be well mounted. When he was not fighting he used to ride every morning from 7.30 to 9.30, winter and summer, whatever the weather—but unlike Haig he never rode at all during the four years of the First World War. In 1919, at the age of sixty-seven as Supreme Allied Commander, he headed the victory procession in Paris through the Arc de Triomphe, wearing the uniform of a Marshal of France and riding a magnificent black thoroughbred horse.

Foch was originally commissioned into the Artillery—Napoleon's own arm—in 1873 and was promoted captain in 1878. He married in 1883 and gained admission to the École Superieure de Guerre in Paris (the French Staff College) two years later. In 1890 he was summoned to the Ministry of War to join the Third Bureau of General Staff (the 'Operations' Branch dealing with war plans). In 1895 he was appointed Assistant Professor of Military History, Strategy and Applied Tactics at the École Superieure de Guerre. This was his decisive opportunity. It was in teaching others that he learnt about the art of war himself. Foch took the framework of his philosophical study of the elements of war direct from Clausewitz, who, as the teacher of the Prussian Army, had become the recognised master in the eyes of military Europe. Clausewitz proclaimed the sovereign virtue of the will to conquer and the unique value of the offensive carried out with unlimited violence by a nation in arms. In his view, to overthrow the main enemy in battle was the primary object of all military strategy. For Foch 'the will to conquer' became even more important than tactics itself. He always taught that a battle is never lost unless it is acknowledged to be lost. And he was more concerned to fortify his own will and that of his fellow commanders than to weaken the will of the opposing commanders.

In 1908 Foch was appointed Commandant of the École de Guerre. It was in the following year that Brigadier-General Henry Wilson, Commandant of the British Staff College at Camberley, came to call on him, his object being to study the methods of the École and its commandant. They very soon formed an alliance and began to discuss the role of a British Expeditionary Force in the event of a war with Germany. Foch then paid a return visit to Wilson in England. When Wilson left Camberley in 1910 and became Director of Military Operations at the War Office their liaison continued. It gradually strengthened with further visits by Wilson to French commanders and chiefs of staff until Britain was virtually committed to land an expeditionary force to operate on the left wing of the French armies on the outbreak of war. The famous French Plan XVII was based on an immediate offensive *à outrance* by four French armies: the 1st and 2nd in Lorraine towards the Saar, which was the right attack, while the left attack was the 3rd Army opposite Metz and the 5th Army—on the left of which was the BEF—facing the Ardennes, with the 4th Army in strategic reserve. Thus some 800,000 French troops, revelling in their highly coloured uniforms, were launched towards the lost French territories, with their objective the Rhine. The idea was to dislocate the ponderous German war machine before it could get started.

The German Schlieffen Plan was to knock out France whilst Russia was still mobilising. The weight of the French Army was to be lured towards the Rhine whilst the main German force thrust rapidly through Belgium to outflank the French. From the German point of view the French plan was perfect and played straight into their hands—particularly as the French armies attacked with such reckless bravery. In the two weeks that the Battle of the Frontiers lasted, the French lost over 300,000 men and nearly 5,000 officers. The 2nd Army, which included Foch's 20 Corps, was very severely handled.

It was at this time that Colonel Max Weygand was appointed to Foch's staff and these two formed a relationship which became one of the most famous in military history. Weygand's slight physique and insignificant features and presence disguised great force of character, high powers of organisation and an amazing memory. Foch and Weygand were entirely complementary to one another and between them there was absolute trust, loyalty and confidence—the perfect ingredients for a successful partnership between a commander and his chief of staff.

When the counter-offensive of the Marne started Foch was given command of the 9th Army, in which he much distinguished himself—so much so that he was summoned to Joffre's head-quarters and given control of Castelnau's and Maud'huy's armies and ordered to co-ordinate their moves with those of the British and Belgian armies. Foch made a great impression on Sir John French, the Commander-in-Chief of the BEF and also on Haig, with both of whom he became closely concerned at this time. Then, towards the end of 1916, both Foch and Joffre were removed from their high appointments and the latter was superseded by General Nivelle. Foch was allowed to keep his empty title of Army Group Commander but was in fact relegated to the chair-manship of an advisory committee to study problems of strategy in Paris.

Foch was then sixty-five and it was typical of the man and his mentality that he did not for a moment contemplate retirement or inactivity. He regarded this as an interim period in his life, in which he could 'reculer pour mieux sauter'. He set about increasing his physical fitness by much hard walking, and a great deal of deep thinking—not about the past but about the future.

Painlevé, the French Minister of War, who had not been in favour of Nivelle's appointment, or his offensive plan, was a great admirer of Foch and soon extracted him from the backwoods and sent him on an important mission to Italy to discuss with Cadorna, the Italian Commander-in-Chief, how French and British reinforcements could be used should the Italian Army be in need of them. But Foch then had to return to his sinecure appointment in Paris.

Within a few months Nivelle, his grand offensive having failed completely, was dismissed as Commander-in-Chief of the French Army on 11 May 1917 and replaced by Pétain. But this change came too late to avert a serious mutiny which spread through the greater part of the French Army. On 10 May Foch was summoned by Painlevé, told that Pétain was to succeed Nivelle, and offered the job of Chief of the General Staff in Paris. Foch would have much preferred to have had a command in the field but both Pétain and Painlevé urged him to accept this most important staff appointment as his prestige was so high with the Allies. In actual fact this appointment gained Foch increased prestige and greater influence in the conduct of the war even than that of the commander-in-chief in the field.

On being appointed supreme commander of the Allied armies in France, Foch's first action was to impress on both the French and British armies that the all-important task for the moment was for the troops engaged in battle to hold their ground. Only then would it be possible to relieve formations which had suffered heavily and think of counter-measures.

On 23 March Ludendorff launched an attack on Arras which completely failed to penetrate the defences of Byng's 3rd Army. On this day Pershing visited Foch's headquarters and pledged all his troops to him. There were now 300,000 American troops in France, forming eight divisions, of which three were already in the line. Next day Foch, who appeared buoyant and at the top of his form, visited Haig and told him that he wanted to create two strong groups of reserves, one on either flank of the enemy's bulge, with a view to a counter-attack.

Foch always paid particular attention to his reserves. One of his first principles of war was never to be afraid to use reserves but, having done so, always to build up some more. In the conditions which existed on the Western Front, where the adversaries were

L

evenly balanced, Foch did not believe in attempting a break-through as did Haig and Ludendorff. He always tried to draw in the enemy's reserves before committing his own. Ludendorff's offensive created huge pockets which at once became vulnerable to Foch's counter-offensives.

One of Foch's favourite precepts was *sureté* (protection). He liked always to operate from a secure base—if he could. Another was: 'De quoi s'agit-il?' (What is the problem?) This was perhaps Foch's favourite question and he posed it frequently to himself, to his colleagues and to his subordinate commanders. Once he could get the object clearly established, all the factors to be con-sidered in its attainment fell into place. Foch liked to establish his headquarters on the Montgomery pattern, rather than the Haig pattern. He preferred it to be small and inconspicuous, not a place of entertainment but one of quiet contemplation. Foch was always supremely confident in the outcome of the operations, though he was never boastful.

On 4 April at Beauvais Lloyd George had asked Foch whose hand he would prefer to be playing at that time—his own or Ludendorff's (Lloyd George, *Memoirs*, Vol V). Foch promised to let him know when he had been able to look into the whole posi-tion and had had time to weigh the resources of the rival armies. On 17 April Lloyd George received a message from Foch which ran as follows: 'If he had to choose between playing his own hand and that of Ludendorff, then, if he had to get to Berlin, he would prefer Ludendorff's hand, but as his mission was to beat Luden-dorff, he would prefer his own.'

Meanwhile the German offensives continued. On 9 April they attacked with nine divisions in a sector held by only three divisions of the British 1st Army (Horne), the centre one of which was Portuguese. The complete collapse of this division led to the development of a dangerous situation. On the 12th Haig issued his famous 'Backs to the wall' message to his troops. 'Every posi-tion must be held to the last man. With our backs to the wall and believing in the justice of our cause, each one of us must fight on to the end.'

At this time Haig became bitterly critical of Foch. He wanted reserve divisions thrown in at once whereas Foch was always seeking to husband his reserves. But of course there had to be a happy mean between the two or there would have been no position for the reserves to preserve. Eventually, under pressure from Haig, Foch modified his attitude. But these were critical days, with Ludendorff sensing that his last chance of winning the war was slipping away, while the British—and Plumer's army in particular —were feeling that they were nearing the end of their tether. Haig and Plumer were in favour of making a major withdrawal in the Ypres salient. To Foch the idea of surrendering any ground at all was abhorrent. But even Wilson, the British CIGS, began to lose faith in Foch and asked him bluntly whether, if the British were again driven back, he would cover the Channel ports, the bases of the British Army, or protect Paris? Foch replied that the choice didn't arise because he would continue to cover both. But, after several personal visits to British commanders in the line, he realised what a burden they had been carrying and ordered three more reserve divisions to Flanders, making nine in all.

In May there was an interlude; but even Foch realised that, if the German assaults were to continue with increased vigour, the Allied situation might become desperate. His immediate concern was to create fresh reserves to replace those he had committed to any particular sector of the front. For this purpose he proposed to use American troops. Here he and the British and French prime ministers and commanders clashed head-on with the American General Pershing, who was determined to create an all-American army which would only be used as such. This was quite understandable in ordinary circumstances but time and General Ludendorff would not wait—and the arrival of American troops was so much slower than had been hoped. Pershing was very averse to pouring new wine into old bottles—even though the new wine might be untested and untasted. Foch accepted this very pig-headed and unco-operative attitude more easily than did Clemenceau, Lloyd George and Haig. Haig remarked in his diary of 1 May: 'I thought Pershing was very obstinate and stupid. He did not seem to realise the urgency of the situation.'

Later the Americans did agree that, in view of the great emergency their troops would serve, under the general direction of Pershing, in battalions, companies or even platoons in British and French formations.

CHAPTER THIRTEEN

The Allied Counter-offensive: Hamel, the Tank. Allenby in Palestine

By the middle of May the crisis was over. During June and July Foch and Haig began concerting plans for a great Allied counter-offensive. An action took place at Hamel, north-west of Villiers-Bretonneux, on 4 July 1918 by troops of Rawlinson's 4th Army, which marked not only a turning-point in tank warfare but a turning-point in the war itself, which certainly accelerated our final victory. It was an action to which not nearly enough importance has been attached by historians. In fact books on the First World War, and biographies of the commanders therein, have been written in which this action is barely mentioned.

The credit for the success of this action at Hamel must be given primarily to two men, Colonel Fuller and General Rawlinson. Colonel (later Major-General) J. F. C. Fuller, who was chief of staff to the Tank Corps at the time, was one of the pioneers of tank warfare and certainly one of the most brilliant brains in the British Army. He had been trying to impress upon all the Allied commanders the merits of the new Mark V tank which was being produced in England in large numbers at the beginning of 1918, and he found Winston Churchill a great ally in their production and distribution. Foch and Pétain too were convinced of their possibilities. However, Fuller found Haig, for whose methods he had little admiration, very slow to see the advantages of this new weapon. He found Rawlinson, commanding the 4th Army, much more receptive—despite the fact that his Australians had had bitter experience of the earlier type of tank in the battle of Bulle-court on 11 April 1917 and the very name 'tank' was anathema to them.

Rawlinson was always seeking to solve the problem of the trench barrier. Bombardment and assault had been tried at Neuve Chapelle; gas and assault at Loos; then the long-drawn-out battles of attrition on the Somme and at Passchendaele. Always there had been the difficulty of achieving surprise, the casualties had been catastrophic and the results had been disappointing. The tank attack at Cambrai had shown that the long preliminary bombardment, which destroyed all chance of surprise, was not an essential preliminary to attack; but the tanks of 1916 and 1917 had certain structural defects which could only have been over-come as a result of experience of their employment in action.

Rawlinson had selected as the launching day for the attack American Independence Day (4 July) as it was the first occasion on which American troops—four companies of the 33rd American Division—were to take part alongside British troops. At the very last moment General Pershing had informed Rawlinson that no American troops were to be employed. However, this message arrived too late for them to be withdrawn. They fought splendidly and didn't have too many casualties, so all was well. Perhaps Rawlinson, like Nelson, had turned a blind eye to Pershing's signal. As the Australians had no confidence in tanks, Rawlinson had arranged for them to practise with the new Mark V tank daily. The commanders of the two Australian divisions in the Australian Corps were Major-General Sinclair MacClagan (4th Division) and Major-General Sir Neville Maskelyne Smyth, VC (2nd Division). The latter had made a great reputation for himself in command of the 1st Australian Brigade in Gallipoli.

The objectives of this 4 July 1918 attack were Hamel and Ovaire woods and the high ground east of these localities. In order to reduce casualties it was decided that as few infantry and as many tanks as possible were to be employed. There were only two and a half brigades of infantry, that is ten battalions in all, sixty fighting tanks and four supply tanks. The artillery preparation was based on the employment of 326 field guns and 302 heavy guns. No preliminary bombardment was to precede the attack; the covering barrage and counter-battery fire were to open at zero hour. This was fixed for 3.10 am, when the infantry advance would start. The tanks assembled behind the infantry; their engines were started at 2.59 am and at 3.02 am they moved forward and advanced with the leading wave of infantry behind the artillery barrage. For two hours before dawn aircraft were constantly overhead to drown the noise of the tanks' engines.

By 5 am the attack was over. The Germans put up a good fight but they were surprised and overwhelmed, first by the wall of artillery fire which suddenly descended on them, and then by the sudden arrival of the tanks. The British artillery did well in their counter-battery work so that the attackers were not troubled by German counter-battery fire. The tanks returned in triumph, carrying the cheering wounded on their backs. The usual difficulty of getting ammunition and supplies forward was solved by parachute drops from aircraft and by the supply tanks, which delivered barbed wire, screw pickets, corrugated iron, hand grenades, ammunition and drinking water (plus a good unofficial dollop of Scotch whisky and rum!). Thus, instead of the infantry having to advance laden like beasts of burden, as they had done on the Somme, they were able to go into the attack in fighting order.

General Fuller wrote in his book, *The Memoirs of an Unconventional Soldier* (and what an unconventional soldier he was!):

In rapidity, brevity and completeness of success no battle of the war can compare with Hamel. The economies were remarkable: the total Australian losses, killed and wounded, were only 672; of the sixty tanks fifty-eight reached their objectives and fifty-five returned to their rallying points; and the five which were disabled were salvaged by the night 6/7 July. Of the tank personnel no single officer or man was killed and only thirteen Other Ranks were wounded, and of these five only slightly.

Even though the Mark IV tank was less handy than the Mark V there was no reason why, with the twelve battalions of tanks we had, we should not have carried out several such raids between 1 January and 15 March 1918, in which case the German offensive of 22 March might well have been upset. Though we did not realise it at the time I realised it now that on 3 July 1918 we were no more than a poor street singer and on the 4th this singer was standing on the stage of a great opera house deafened by applause.

The news of Hamel got around and was a tremendous morale-raiser. But Fuller criticises Haig very severely for preferring to maintain the strength of horsed cavalry rather than expand the Tank Corps. He says in his book (p 340 ff), referring to Haig:

It is indeed strange that this man whose stubbornness had all but ruined us on the Somme should, from August 1918 onwards become the driving force of the Allied Armies. Yet this was so, and it must stand to his credit; for no man can deny that, during the last hundred days of the war his spirit fitted events as a hand fits a glove. Yet to me it is stranger still that these events were created not by him or by his ideas but by the tank and in no small part by my ideas. The machine which he could not understand, which he intuitively loathed and which he would gladly have abolished altogether, made him one of the outstanding figures of the war. Yet to me, strangest of all is it that I, who considered him, and still consider him, one of, if not the, most unimaginative and unseeing of Generals who has ever commanded a British Army, a man whose Stone-age ideas I had fought tooth and nail, should, since December 1916, have played so great a part in this his apotheosis. It would be incorrect to say that I made the tank, for I fashioned its tactics only; but it is strictly and historically correct to say that the tank made Lord Haig.

Early in August 1918 Clemenceau informed Foch that he had been made a Marshal of France, the highest honour his country could confer upon him. And it served as a great spur to him in his endeavours to achieve final victory.

Meanwhile the final preparations had been made for the great offensive of Rawlinson's 4th Army in front of Amiens. With the greatest secrecy his army had been doubled in strength to thirteen divisions. The main stroke was to be made by the splendid Australian and Canadian Corps. An hour before sunrise on that fateful (for the Germans) 8 August, 450 tanks crawled forward, shrouded by thick mist. Only then did 2,000 British guns open fire, making a devastated area of the German trenches. Only north of the Somme, where there were few tanks, was there a partial check. General Fuller can be excused his exuberance. All his dreams, his training and his urging had paid off. And so, with Foch's inspiring call, 'tout le monde à la bataille', the Allied assault gained momentum until within two months the Germans were suing for an armistice and complete Allied victory was gained. And in this last hundred days of the Great War, though the inspiration was Foch's, the driving force was Haig's.

In the final stage of the war the British armies, with their left next to the Belgians at Dunkirk, were disposed as follows: Plumer, Birdwood, Horne, Byng, Rawlinson—who connected up with the French general's 1st Army south of the Somme. These five men were all splendid and inspiring leaders.

After the war Douglas Haig gave his great prestige and a lot of the energy of his declining years to the creation of the British Legion (in 1921). In 1919 he had been created an earl and voted the sum of £100,000 by Parliament. Soon after this he received a gift which he valued far more highly. A national subscription was raised to purchase a present for him—Bemersyde, the ancestral home of the Haigs, which at the time was in the possession of another branch of the family. Here he spent the last, and perhaps some of the happiest days of his life, amongst the people and the scenery he knew and loved so well.

On 29 January 1928 he died suddenly from a heart attack at the age of sixty-six. His death was the occasion of a remarkable manifestation of national sorrow. He may or may not have been a great general in the mould of Marlborough or Wellington, but he was certainly a very great soldier, with outstanding qualities of heart and mind and tremendous endurance and determination, who served his country well throughout a period of greatest peril.

Foch remained active until 1928 (his seventy-seventh year), when he received news of Haig's death; and, though he had been advised by his doctors to take things easy in the Riviera sunshine, he unhesitatingly set out for London for the funeral ceremonies. On the night of 29 January he was striken by a heart attack and he died on 20 March of that year. Three days later his body was carried to lie alongside the 'Unknown Soldier' beneath the Arc de Triomphe. It was then borne to Notre-Dame and laid in a vault beside Napoleon's grave under the great dome of Les Invalides. Perhaps, to Foch, this would have been his greatest triumph and his heart's desire.

The war on the Western Front had taken a terrible toll. The casualties (*vide* the Official Casualty Returns) were tremendous. To take first the British: the casualties suffered on the opening day of the Somme battle (1 July 1916) were 61,816 and easily exceeded the battle casualties in the Crimean War, the Boer War and the Korean War put together. For the whole month of July 1916 they were 196,081. In no other month were there so many, though in eight other months they exceeded 100,000. Those months were September 1916 (Somme), 115,056; April 1917 (Arras), 120,070; October 1917 (Passchendaele), 119,808; March 1918 (German offensive), 173,721; April 1918, 143,168; August 1918, 122,272; September 1918, 114,831; October 1918, 121,046. The total British casualties on the Western Front were 2,706,150. The French total was 4,938,000 and the Germans lost 3,088,743. So the Allied casualties were more than double those of the Germans.

The Palestine campaign provided General Allenby with the opportunity of using cavalry in open country, which Sir John French and Sir Douglas Haig had hoped for in the West but had never been able to effect. Certainly in Palestine the opportunity provided the man—or perhaps the man provided the opportunity. In his thorough attention to matters of administration, his brilliant planning, and his bold execution, Allenby showed himself to be the perfect commander in those particular circumstances. And the use he made of Lawrence and the Arabs was indeed a masterly illustration of how a regular soldier can adapt his thinking, and the principles on which he had been brought up in the Army from his Sandhurst days, to an unusual character and unusual methods.

In a sense Allenby can be considered the luckiest British general of the First World War because, having served on the Western Front during the first two years of the war as a divisional, corps and army commander, in conditions where leadership was at a discount, he found himself in conditions where leadership was everything. Allenby was essentially a leader, and was not particularly distinguished as a slide-rule planner living in a château behind the lines. He was also lucky that, because he was not *persona grata* with Haig, in June 1917 the CIGS, General Robertson, recommended him for the Palestine Command.

Edmund Allenby was born on 23 April 1861 and was thus fifty-three when the war started. He had the usual upbringing of a successful soldier of his time—Sandhurst and the Staff College, Camberley—and he had served in the South African War. He had been originally gazetted to the 6th Inniskilling Dragoons and later commanded the 5th Lancers. From 1905 to 1909 he commanded 4 Cavalry Brigade and from 1910 to 1914, as a major-general, he was Inspector-General of Cavalry. In the early days of the war in France Allenby commanded a cavalry division and then the Cavalry Corps. When General Plumer took over command of the 2nd Army from Smith-Dorrien, Allenby was given command, first of 5 Corps and then of the 3rd Army.

When Allenby took over the so-called Eastern Force in Palestine he had three mounted divisions (Anzac, Australian and Yeomanry) and four infantry divisions—52nd, 53rd, 54th, 74th—of which the first three were first-line Territorial divisions which had fought in Gallipoli, while the 74th was formed from dismounted Yeomanry units. In addition the 60th (London) Division, made up from second-line TA battalions, which had fought in France and Salonika, was arriving from that country, and another, the 75th Division, was being formed in Egypt from Territorial and Indian Army battalions. In August 1917 Allenby organised them into three corps—the Desert Mounted Corps under General Chauvel (an Australian), 20 Corps under Sir Philip Chetwode, and 21 Corps under Sir Edward Bulfin.

Allenby was universally known in the Army as 'The Bull'. He was given this nickname from his appearance and bearing— he was a big, strong man with a firm jaw and a somewhat arrogant expression. He also had a volcanic temper—though he was incapable of meanness or pettiness. He electrified his troops by dashing about in a car—on the Montgomery pattern—and impressing his personality upon them in indelible fashion in a way which was quite impossible on the Western Front.

Allenby's campaigns ended with the capture of Jerusalem and then in the complete defeat of the Turks. The steps taken by Allenby to deceive the Turks as to his intentions were varied, ingenious and completely successful. In the final stages of his campaign the Arabs, under Lawrence, played an important part. But it was Allenby's own tremendous drive and determination and the bold use of his mounted troops which brought him overwhelming victory. Few generals have carried out the pursuit of a beaten enemy with such relentless determination. During the last six weeks of his campaign his Army had advanced 350 miles and captured 75,000 prisoners, for the loss of only 5,000 casualties.

In 1919 Allenby received the thanks of Parliament, £50,000, promotion to field-marshal and a viscountcy from a grateful country. To be fair to the distinguished army commanders on the Western Front, it must be admitted that they had a much harder row to hoe. They had a much tougher, better armed and better commanded enemy—and not anything like the opportunity which Allenby had for dynamic leadership. Nevertheless all credit must be given to Allenby for making the best use of the particular conditions he had to face and using them to his best advantage.

And so the land victories in the West and in Palestine were gained, to a considerable extent, through the use of mobile arms— the tank and the cavalry. This was the swan song of the latter but only the comparatively early development of the former. Had the war continued into 1919 plans had been made for a great Allied offensive based on the formation of an enormous armoured force of three tank groups, each consisting of three tank brigades, each of four battalions. The British armoured force in 1919 would have been the equivalent of seven armoured divisions of 1939–45 and the supply echelons were to consist of 10,000 Ford cross-country tractors, in order that the depth of advance of the armoured force should not be limited. And just over twenty years later we were to see the tanks—which we had invented—used in their maturity in the way that General Fuller and other tank experts had advised and foretold—but by the Germans. This came about, not as some people thought, by any negligence or lack of foresight on the part of our British military leaders, but purely and simply because the British people and their governments were not prepared to pay for their security in peacetime. If they had, it is possible that the Second World War might never have started.

One of the most famous VCs of all was Captain and Brevet-major (Acting Lieut-Colonel) Viscount John Standish Surtees Predergast Vereker Gort, DSO and two bars, MVO, MC, who won his VC with the 1st Battalion Grenadier Guards at Canal du Nord, France, on 27 September 1918. He won an MC and a DSO and two bars, besides the Victoria Cross, and was an intrepid leader of troops in battle. His VC citation ran as follows:

For most conspicuous bravery, skilful leading and devotion to duty during the attack of the Guards Division across the Canal du Nord, when in command of the 1st Battalion Grenadier Guards, the leading battalion of the 3rd Guards Brigade. Although wounded, and under heavy artillery and machine gun fire, when the battalion was held up he went across open ground and obtained the assistance of a tank, which he personally led and directed to the best possible advantage. In so doing he was again severely wounded by a shell. Notwithstanding considerable loss of blood, after lying on a stretcher for a while, he insisted on getting up and personally directing the attack, as a result of which his battalion captured 200 prisoners, two batteries of field guns and numerous machine guns. Colonel Gort refused to leave the field until he had seen the success signal go up on the final objective.

Four days after Gort had won his VC a very distinguished Canadian, Lieutenant Milton Fowler Gregg, won his at Cambrai, France, with the Royal Canadian Regiment, the Nova Scotia Regiment. He won the MC at Lens in 1917, a bar to his MC at Arras in 1918 and the Victoria Cross in October of the same year. When the advance of his brigade was held up by fire from both flanks and by thick uncut wire, he crawled forward alone and found a small gap in the wire through which he led his men and forced an entry into the enemy trench. The enemy counter-attacked in force and, through lack of bombs, the situation became critical. Although wounded Gregg returned alone under heavy fire and collected a further supply. Then, in spite of being wounded a second time, he led his men forward with the greatest determination and cleared the enemy trenches. He personally killed or wounded eleven of the enemy and took twenty-five prisoners and captured twelve machine-guns. He remained with his company, despite his wounds, and two days later led his men in a further attack until he was severely wounded.

Although the war with Germany had come to an end in 1918, fighting was still going on elsewhere. Ill-judged though it may have been, the campaign in North Russia presented difficult and dangerous conditions, very different from those on the Western Front. Five VCs were awarded in 1919, after the Armistice with Germany, for gallantry in North Russia. Three were gained by officers of the Royal Navy in Kronstadt Harbour, and two by the 45th Battalion Royal Fusiliers during the campaign.

Lieutenant Agar, RN, was born on 4 January 1890 at Kandy in Ceylon. He entered the Royal Navy in May 1905. He served with the Grand Fleet in 1914 and 1915, and in Gallipoli in 1915 where he was present at the evacuation. In 1917 and 1918 he served in North Russia in HMS *Iphigenia*. In 1918 he was employed by the Admiralty for special service in coastal motor-boats; and in 1919 he served in the Baltic in coastal motor-boats under the

Foreign Office. Lieutenant Agar's citation in the *London Gazette* of 22 August 1919 merely states: 'in recognition of his conspicuous gallantry, coolness and skill under extremely difficult conditions in action'. But, of course, at the time the whole operation was very secret.

In 1919 the coastal motor-boat was the Navy's new weapon. The essence of these boats was speed and by reason of their shallow draught they were able to skim over our own, and the enemy's, minefields. The boats were therefore especially suitable for attacking ships in well-defended harbours. Their crews consisted of specially selected young naval officers. The story of how Agar, in HM Coastal Motor Boat No 4, sank the 7,000-ton Bolshevik armoured cruiser *Oleg* in Kronstadt harbour on the night of 17 June is an epic of the sea and won for him the Victoria Cross and for the two members of his crew, Acting Sub-Lieutenant Hampsheir, RNVR, and Chief Mechanic Beeley, RNVR, the DSC and the Conspicuous Gallantry Medal respectively. Six days later Agar was awarded the DSO for his attack on Kronstadt naval harbour when in command of HM Coastal Motor Boat No 7.

A dramatic story lies behind this achievement. Agar had been training with the Coastal Motor Boats at Osea Island when he was ordered to go on a very secret mission to Finland under the aegis of the British Secret Service. The Russian frontier was now closed against the Allies and the lines of communication bringing news through various 'couriers' across the frontier had broken down. It was essential to restore these links. It was thought that a possible solution would be for the Coastal Motor Boats to cross the narrow Gulf of Finland and land the couriers on the coast of Estonia, whence they could make their way to Petrograd and on to Moscow. Agar's team consisted of six in all, in two Coastal Motor Boats. It was while on this very complicated and secret mission that the opportunity came of penetrating the naval harbour of Kronstadt and sinking a Russian cruiser.

The large fortress of Krasnaya Gorka dominated the southern entrance to the Gulf of Finland, and the garrison, believing that the White Russian Army of General Yudenitch had begun its march on Petrograd from the Estonian frontier, revolted against its Red commissars and hoisted the White Russian flag. It was of course a key position. But it was feared on the Allied side that Russian warships would bombard Krasnaya Gorka and that nothing could be done to held the defenders. This bombardment soon began.

The temptation for Agar to start that night and attack the bombarding ships was very great: but his obligation to his own secret mission came first. He managed to contact the British admiral at Bjorko and asked him to get a message through to his intelligence chief. The answer came back that his CMBs were to be used only for intelligence purposes unless specially directed by the flag officer. The admiral told Agar that he would not *direct* him to attack, but that he would give him every support if he did so.

The two CMBs set off that night and all went well at first; but the second CMB, No 7, under Sub-Lieutenant J. Sindell, RNR, hit some obstacle and damaged her propellor shaft. So the expedition had to be abandoned and No 7 CMB towed back to their secret base. But as Krasnaya Gorka was still under heavy bombardment Agar decided to attack by himself in No 4 CMB on the following night. Agar's party had been sent to Finland with false passports and in civilian clothes. But they had been allowed to take their naval uniforms with them in the boats. Now, for the attack, they discarded their civilian clothes, put on their naval uniforms and flew the White Ensign.

No 4 CMB, with her three-man crew, arrived off Tolboukin Lighthouse on the approaches to Kronstadt harbour without incident. Agar had everything ready to discharge his torpedo except for removing the 'stops'. He crept slowly ahead, passing close to two destroyers. Then he motioned to Lieut Hampsheir to remove the safety pin from the cartridge in the firing chamber. Unfortunately, in doing so Hampsheir accidentally fired it. There was a hard shudder throughout the boat and he expected the torpedo to go: but luckily the 'stops' were down and held her safe in the trough where the fish lay. This was a setback, made worse by the choppy sea. It takes both time and patience to insert another cartridge and reload in the dark; and at any moment they might be discovered in the light of the constant gun flashes. After a nerve-wracking age of waiting, the job was done. Agar increased speed. They were soon through the screen and in position. He fired at the centre of the *Oleg*'s three funnels and once clear of the torpedo increased to full speed, turned round and made towards the Estonian coast, hoping to mislead the enemy as to where they had come from. Within a minute there was a thick column of black smoke from the *Oleg*. Gun flashes came from all directions from the forts and the destroyers. The shells threw up columns of water round the CMB, soaking Agar and his crew to the skin, but they got clean away.

The White Russian commandant was incredulous that Agar could have sunk the *Oleg*. 'How could you, in such a fragile craft, single-handed attack and destroy a large armoured cruiser of over 7,000 tons?' he asked. Agar could see that he was perplexed and unconvinced. A Finnish officer offered him a seat in a small aeroplane, piloted by a young Swedish pilot, to go and look at the scene of the exploit. Agar jumped at the offer. He was thrilled to get a bird's-eye view of the area of their great adventure. The plane came down to 2,000ft above the spot where the *Oleg* had been anchored. And there she was, lying on her side at the bottom of the sea, looking like an enormous dead whale. Agar wrote: 'It is a curious feeling to observe one's victim and I must confess quite candidly that I had no sensation of joy or elation.' But as they turned to the west and flew over the fortress of Krasnaya Gorka they saw the Red flag flying instead of the White one. Relief had come too late. The fortress had capitulated.

A British naval signal dated 26 January 1919 was brief and to the point. It ran as follows: 'For sinking the Bolshevik cruiser *Oleg* H.M. The King has been pleased to make the following awards. To Lieut. Agar RN, Victoria Cross. To Acting Sub-Lieut. Hampsheir RNVR, Distinguished Service Cross. To Chief M. M. Beeley RNVR, Conspicuous Gallantry Medal.'

Leadership, leadership, leadership, what a thing it is—more to be desired than gold and much more valuable. The examples I have given in this book on the part of many different men, of all ranks and of all arms of the Services, have one thing in common—

M

a rising of the human spirit over doubt, despair, fear, hardship, strain and fatigue and great danger to life itself, man's most precious possession. The best definition of leadership lies in the lives and experiences of such men.

Bibliography

Agar, Augustus. *Footprints in the Sea* (Cahill, 1959)

Barrow, General Sir George. *The Life of Sir Charles Monro* (Hutchinson, 1931)

Blake, Robert (ed). *The Private Papers of Douglas Haig* (Eyre & Spottiswoode, 1952)

Bonham-Carter, Victor. *Soldier True: The Life of Field-Marshal Sir William Robertson* (Muller, 1963)

Carew, Tim. *Wipers* (Hamish Hamilton, 1974)

Churchill, Sir Winston. *The World Crisis 1916–18* (Thornton Butterworth, 1927)

Colville, J. R. *Man of Valour: Field-Marshal Lord Gort* (Collins, 1972)

Connell, John. *Wavell: Soldier and Scholar* (Collins, 1964)

Cooper, Duff. *Haig* (Faber, undated)

Coppard, George. *With a Machine Gun to Cambrai* (HMSO, 1969)

Edmonds, Brigadier Sir James. *Military Operations in France and Belgium* (Macmillan, 1933)

Essame, H. *The Battle for Europe 1918* (Batsford, 1972)

Falls, Cyril. *Marshal Foch* (Blackie, 1939)

——. *The First World War* (Longmans, 1960)

Fuller, Major-General J. F. C. *The Memoirs of an Unconventional Soldier* (Ivor Nicholson & Watson, 1936)

——. *Tanks in the Great War*

Gilbert, Martin. *Winston Churchill*, Vol III *1914–16* (Heinemann, 1972)

Hart, Liddell. *Foch: The Man of Orleans* (Eyre & Spottiswoode, 1931)

Maurice, Major-General Sir Frederick (ed). *The Life of Lord Rawlinson of Trent* (Cassell, 1928)

Merewether, Lieut-Colonel, and Smith, F. E. *The Indian Corps in France* (Murray, 1919)

Middlebrook, Martin. *The First Day of the Somme* (Allen Lane, the Penguin Press, 1971)

Neame, Lieut-General Sir Philip. *Playing with Strife* (Harrap, 1947)

Smith-Dorrien, Sir Horace. *Memoirs of Forty-Eight Years Service* (Murray, 1925)

Smyth, Sir John. *The Only Enemy* (Hutchinson, 1959)

——. *Sandhurst: The History of the RMA and the RMC* (Weidenfeld & Nicolson, 1961)

——. *The Story of the Victoria Cross* (Muller, 1963)

——. *The Valiant* (Mowbray, 1970)

——. *In This Sign Conquer: The Story of the Army Chaplains* (Mowbray, 1968)

Spears, Major-General Sir Edward. *Two Men Who Saved France* (Eyre & Spottiswoode, 1966)

Terraine, John. *Mons: the Retreat to Victory* (Batsford, 1960)

War Memoirs of David Lloyd George (Ivor Nicholson & Watson, 1939)

Wavell, Sir Archibald. *Allenby: A Study in Greatness* (Harrap, 1940)

Acknowledgements

When the First World War ended and the Staff College courses at Camberley and Quetta restarted, the instructors and pupils for some years consisted of officers who had been much involved with the campaigns of that war, about which I am writing in this book. During my two years as a pupil at Camberley in 1923–4 we discussed the campaigns of the First World War and sought to derive from them lessons which were likely to be of advantage to us in future wars. Naturally, during our two years together we exchanged views and experiences with our fellow teachers and students, and I am grateful to them for their influence upon my own military thinking.

In the writing of this book I am particularly grateful to General Sir Reginald Savory, who was brought up with me in the Indian Army, for his account of leadership in Gallipoli from a subaltern's point of view; and to General Sir Philip Neame, VC, who had been one of my teachers at Camberley, who allowed me to quote from his book, *Playing with Strife*. During my time as a military correspondent in the latter years of the Second World War I made friends with that famous military writer, Basil Liddell Hart (later Sir Basil) and had many discussions with him on the tactics and strategy of the First World War, about which he had written so brilliantly. Between us we helped to initiate the Military Commentator's Circle, of which he became President.

As always I would like to thank my old friend, Mr D. W. King, OBE, FLA, for many years the Chief Librarian of the Ministry of Defence Library (Central and Army), and his successor, Mr J. C. Andrews, and his capable and helpful assistants, who have been towers of strength to me in providing the books and documents I required. I am most grateful also to Dr Noble Frankland, Director of the Imperial War Museum, and his staff, for their invaluable help.

Lastly, I would once again like to give my warmest thanks to my wife, Frances, who has typed so much of the twenty-nine books I have written and done such valuable sub-editing as well; and to my excellent secretaries, Jacqueline Stead and Penelope Hill, who have been so helpful over this book.

JACKIE SMYTH

Index